MAKE FUNNY

MORE TALES OF ADVENTURE, TRAVEL AND LIFE

GEORGE MAHOOD

Contents

Copyright	VI
The Banoffee Pie Saga	1
A Weekend in Cornwall with Storm Kathleen	17
The Tesco Car Park Marathon	33
The Cat Next Door	43
A Jog in a Bog	58
Tour de France - Part One	78
The Kingfisher - Part Five	88
Tour de France - Part Two	97
Making Dreams Come True in Yellow and Blue	107
Tour de France - Part Three	119
The Dog Next Door	130
Tour de France - Part Four	144

Tales from a Conference Centre	158
Two Months Alcohol-Free	175
In It for the Long Run	183
Welly Wanging, Waterfalls, and Wayward Golf Balls	195
The Dog Next Door - Part Two	207
The Choosing	213
The Hornet Dilemma	232
The Dog Next Door - Part Three	240
Make Funny	247
What Happens in Poznań, Stays in Poznań...	253
Lessons Learned from Ten Years as a Full-Time Author	269
Stay Connected with Reconnecting...	276
Reconnecting...	277
Also by George Mahood	278
Acknowledgements	280

Copyright © 2024 by George Mahood

All rights reserved. This book or any portion thereof may not be reproduced or used in any manner whatsoever without the express written permission of the author except for the use of brief quotations in a book review.
This edition published 2024 by George Mahood.
georgemahood.substack.com/

www.facebook.com/georgemahood
www.instagram.com/georgemahood
www.tiktok.com/@georgemahood
www.twitter.com/georgemahood

www.georgemahood.com

The Banoffee Pie Saga

During my teenage years, Damian was the only member of our friendship group who lived within walking distance of Northampton town centre. The rest of us were scattered across the surrounding villages, separated by unreliable bus routes and taxi fares that were far beyond our budgets.

After nights out at Northampton's Roadmender – a haven for underage revellers thanks to its 'relaxed' door policy – a group of us would usually stagger back to Damo's parents' house to sleep. We ended the night sat around the kitchen table, eating whatever we could find in the fridge (typically big stacks of ham, cheese and his mum's weird crispbread things).

On one particularly drunken night, Damo dropped a bombshell: 'Did you know my grandma invented banoffee pie?'

Or at least, that's the version etched into our collective memory. We all erupted into laughter at the absurdity and audacity of his claim, and carried on stuffing our faces with crispbreads.

To those unfamiliar with banoffee pie, it's a popular dessert pie made from bananas, cream and caramel sauce.

Damo denies ever making this bold statement, but for some reason it stuck and the story of Damo's grandma's banana-and-toffee-flavoured contribution to world cuisine has been a regular source of entertainment for our group of friends ever since.

The more we repeated it, the more it riled Damo. So the more we repeated it. I don't even know why we found it so funny. It's not even a particularly outlandish claim. Somebody had to have first created banoffee pie. Why not Damo's grandma?

This was about 30 years ago and it still gets mentioned regularly within our circle of friends.

Damian eventually learned it was easier just to give in to our taunts and go along with the joke, rather than try to resist it.

Damo had a dessert buffet at his wedding, featuring many different flavours of cheesecake. One of them was banoffee pie flavoured. I'd had a few drinks and started telling all the guests that Damo's family received royalties every time anyone ate banoffee pie. The whole lot was demolished in seconds.

Damo at his wedding with banoffee pie cheesecake

He will now often send me pictures whenever he encounters banoffee pie on a menu with a caption like '*just doing my bit for the family business*'. In return, I do the same. Here is a photo I sent him of Rachel and me midway through a 100km run (see *Did Not Believe*).

A banoffee-pie-flavoured bar, midway through the East Devon Round

During my penniless adventure the length of Britain, banoffee pie was mentioned in the guidebook that Ben and I used to navigate from Land's End to John O'Groats.

When I wrote my book - *Free Country* - about the trip, I couldn't resist slipping in a reference to Damo's grandma.

> The route book mentioned that the Bridge of Orchy Hotel served a 'great banoffee pie', which we fantasised about as we cycled past. Incidentally, a very good friend of mine claims that his grandma invented banoffee pie. I don't believe him.
> **Free Country: A Penniless Adventure the Length of Britain**

I've had a look at the menu for the Bridge of Orchy Hotel and there's no mention of banoffee pie on their current menu. That place has clearly gone downhill.

After publishing *Free Country*, I forgot all about the banoffee pie reference until Damo read the book and sent me a text message telling me I was a dick.

I didn't ever expect to write another book. And then *Every Day is a Holiday* came along.

While celebrating *Mom and Pop Business Owner's Day* during my year of holiday celebrations, I bought my wife Rachel a banoffee pie Easter egg from a store in Kettering, so decided to include it after it had stirred a reaction from Damo the first time.

> I was about to buy my pizza when I remembered that it was *Mom and Pop Business Owner's Day*. No disrespect to Tesco, but it is about as far from a Mom and Pop Business as it is possible to get. I put the pizza back and spent 20 minutes driving around Kettering trying to find an independent grocery shop that was open. I then bought the exact same pizza for nearly twice the price, but definitely felt a greater sense of satisfaction. I also purchased a banoffee pie Easter egg for Rachel. My good friend claims that his grandma invented banoffee pie. Despite the fact that I don't believe him, a part of me feels a duty to order it or buy banoffee pie whenever I have the opportunity. I like to think his family are benefiting in some way, through royalties, for each banoffee pie related transaction.
> **Every Day is a Holiday**

Damo read that book too and again sent me a message telling me I was a dick.

When writing *Life's a Beach* - my third book – there were no incidents during those six months of holiday celebrations that featured banoffee pie, so it seemed like I wouldn't be able to complete my hat-trick of references to Damo's grandma. I felt that Damo might now almost be disappointed if I published a book without a mention of banoffee pie and his grandma.

I then had a moment of inspiration. I didn't necessarily need a story involving banoffee pie. I just needed an anecdote connected to Damo, and then the banoffee pie reference could be added as an aside.

> I had promised myself that if we ever moved to Devon, I would buy a surfboard. I was adamant that I wanted to make the most of living near the sea, and for it to feel like a holiday for as long as possible.
> My friend Damo was staying nearby for the week (his grandma apparently invented banoffee pie, don't you know?). He suggested that we hire surfboards one day while he was down, and this seemed like the incentive I needed to buy one. It was also Balance Awareness Week, so surfing seemed as good a way as any to become aware of my balancing.
> I drove to pick up the board from a balding, mildly overweight man in his early forties. He reminded me of me in a few years time, when I will probably realise that buying a surfboard was a silly idea. Still, for the moment I was a surfer. Or, at least, a man with a surfboard.
> **Life's a Beach**

I am now the mildly overweight man in his early (mid) forties. I still have that surfboard. I've used it twice in the last 11 years.

Three books published and three mentions of Damo's grandma inventing banoffee pie.

It had now become a habit.

Damo claimed to be annoyed by it, but I think he was secretly delighted. He admitted that he had bought *Life's a Beach* on Kindle and rather than read the whole thing, he had used the Kindle's search function to look for any mentions of banoffee pie. He then of course sent me a message telling me I was a dick.

Operation Ironman gave me a chance to recount one of my favourite Damo-related stories. One in which I came off very much worse.

> A few years ago I was gorge walking during a friend's stag do in Wales. Gorge walking involves putting on a wetsuit, lifejacket and helmet, and following the course of a river by wading, climbing and swimming along it. We had just jumped off a waterfall into the pool below, and were all sitting around on some rocks at the bottom waiting for everyone to complete the jump. When the last of the group hauled themselves out of the water the instructor announced that it was just a short walk through the woods back to the minibus.
>
> 'WHAT?' shouted my friend Damo, 'I thought we were getting back in the water?'
>
> 'No. This is the end,' I said.
>
> 'But I've just done a piss in my wetsuit.'
>
> 'What, when you were in the water? So what? Everyone does that.'
>
> 'No. Just now. While we've been sitting here on the rocks.'
>
> 'Why did you do that?'

'I was cold and I thought it would warm me up. And I thought we were getting back in the water.'

We all mocked him about this the whole way back to the minibus (and about his claim that his grandma had invented banoffee pie). We were to then get changed into our normal clothes, before being dropped at a pub in Chester for the start of a night out. Damo was first to take his wetsuit off, keen to rid himself of the foul stench of urine. He tossed his soggy wetsuit into the back of the van as we removed our own. I then went to retrieve my jeans, and discovered them wet and stinking underneath his wetsuit in the back of the minibus.

With no other clothes to wear, I was forced to wear the jeans and suffer from wafts of someone else's stale piss from my trousers for the rest of the evening. I have been suspicious of wetsuits ever since.

Operation Ironman: One Man's Four Month Journey from Hospital Bed to Ironman Triathlon

I had a text from Damo back in 2019 saying he had just found *Operation Ironman* on his Kindle and decided to give it a read (it was published in 2015). He then said he was surprised to find he had already read 73%. It turns out 73% was the point in which he and banoffee pie is mentioned. He had bought the book in 2015, searched for banoffee pie, read his section, sent me a text telling me I was a dick, and then didn't pick up the book for another four years.

Banoffee pie was then included in *Not Tonight, Josephine*. I am not certain the dessert Rachel and I had at the gas station on I90 was technically a banoffee pie, but it was definitely a banana-and-toffee-based dessert of some sort.

Our diet in America had been varied and extensive, but lacking in anything green. The restaurant advertised its green salad, which included: avocados, tomatoes, cucumber, sweetcorn, beetroot and a variety of mixed salad leaves.

When it arrived, it looked exactly as described, except it was covered in what appeared to be cooked mince.

'Enjoy your meal,' said the waitress.

'Thank you. Is that mince on top?' I asked.

'Sure is. It's our finest ground beef.'

'Oh, right. I didn't notice that on the menu.'

'It probably ain't on the menu. That's how the chef likes to serve the salad.'

'Ok.'

It seems that everything in middle America, whether you like it or not, is served with beef. And after demolishing my salad in minutes, I think the chef at that gas station on I90 was definitely onto something. I will ask for beef to be added to all my green salads in future.

For dessert, Rachel and I shared a portion of banoffee pie – a dish my friend claims his grandma invented. Fortunately, the chef decided against serving this with minced beef. My friend's grandma would certainly not have approved.

Not Tonight, Josephine: A Road Trip Through Small-Town America

Damo's text message arrived within minutes of me clicking *publish*. He had clearly just skipped to the good bit.

I then published *Travels with Rachel* and managed to continue the streak of now six books.

> We made good progress down the second half of the mountain, thanks to the revolutionary discovery of the path, and arrived back in Aguas Calientes sweatier than either of us had ever been before, which was not ideal preparation for a two-hour train journey.
> With five minutes to spare until our train, I even had time to buy a Peruvian national football shirt from a market trader outside the station. It was a gift for my friend Damo, who claims his grandma invented banoffee pie. We still had a football shirt sized gap in our present bag to fill back at Hostel Royal Frankenstein.
> 'See, I told you we would make it,' I said, giving Rachel a hug.
> 'Don't get too close. I stink.'
> 'Me too. At least we haven't got to sit near each other on the train.'
> **Travels with Rachel: In Search of South America**

There were several opportunities to mention Damo in *How Not to Get Married*. I was best man at Damo's wedding and he was best man at mine. In the end, I chose this story in the section about speeches. His wife Liz has never let him forget this.

> But whoever you thank, the most important person to mention in your speech is your new wife.
> My best friend Damian – who claims his grandma invented banoffee pie – unfortunately missed this im-

portant memo during his speech at his wedding. Well, that's not strictly true. He knew he was supposed to talk about his wife. He even had a beautiful heartfelt tribute to her written down – he's a very caring and sensitive husband – but due to his nerves and being overwhelmed by the occasion, he forgot to read this part during his speech. He thanked his parents. He thanked his best men. He thanked the bridesmaids and the rest of the bridal party. He thanked the band, who hadn't even started performing. He thanked the caterers for cooking such an awesome beef wellington – it was particularly good and fully deserving of a mention. He thanked the florist – she wasn't even there. He thanked the photographer. He thanked the suit hire company. He even thanked the company that provided the portable toilets. But he didn't mention his wife.
How Not to Get Married: A No-Nonsense Guide to Weddings... from a photographer who has seen it all

My short book *Chasing Trails* was released as a freebie, and I wondered if it qualified as a real book and whether I needed to mention banoffee pie. Many people might pick this up having not read any of my other books, and an out-of-place reference to banoffee pie might seem a bit weird. I decided to include one anyway.

Mark was best man at my wedding alongside my other friend Damo (who claims his grandma invented banoffee pie).
Chasing Trails: A Short Fun Book about a Long Miserable Run

My *Did Not Finish* series proved the biggest challenge yet.

It was initially supposed to be one book, detailing various adventures that Rachel and I had undertaken. And one book would only have required one mention of Damo.

The book then kept getting longer and longer until I eventually decided to split it into a series of six shorter books (each one covering about a year) with a seventh published the following year.

Finding seven opportunities to mention Damo's grandma was more difficult than most of the challenges I wrote about in the books. Some of them were a little tenuous but I just about managed it.

> 'What sort of marathon involves being delayed by a wedding?'
> 'A Devon one.'
> We had been in Hope Cove a couple of weeks earlier, meeting up with my friend Damo (who claims his grandma invented banoffee pie) and his family who were holidaying down in Devon. When I told them about our upcoming Salcombe marathon passing through Hope Cove, this was not quite what I envisaged.
> **Did Not Finish: Misadventures in Running, Cycling and Swimming**

> I had been to Barcelona ten years previously on a very drunken stag do and could therefore remember very little about the city. We had stayed for three nights in the worst accommodation in the world. My friend Damo (who claims his grandma invented banoffee

pie) was the best man and had found a hostel that was in a fairly decent location and was very cheap. He emailed me a link to see what I thought. A quick internet search revealed the hostel to have an average rating of 1.5 stars on TripAdvisor, and most of the reviews mentioned the exposed lift shaft, ridiculously unreasonable curfew, and tiny bedrooms with no windows. I replied to Damo saying perhaps it wasn't the best hostel and that maybe there would be a better one. In fact, any other hostel in Barcelona would be a better one. He replied saying, 'too late, I've booked it.'

Did Not Try (Book Two in the DNF Series)

We sat and chatted for about an hour and Doug filled me in on the life stories of the other patients and I told him all about our recent ultramarathon. When visiting time came to an end, I said goodbye to Doug and went and met up with some friends for a curry and a few beers. I stayed the night with my friend Damo (who claims his grandma invented Banoffee Pie), and then drove back down to Devon the following morning.

Did Not Start (Book Three in the DNF Series)

With our camping stuff only just sorted and put away from our holiday in France, it was time to reload the van for a weekend camping in Northampton to celebrate the 40th birthday of my friend Damo (who

claims his grandma invented banoffee pie).
Did Not Sink (Book Four in the DNF Series)

It was a long four-week wait until we could collect Ludo. Christmas provided a much-needed distraction and there was plenty going on with school plays, Christmas fairs, and a big family Christmas to keep our minds from being exclusively occupied with puppy thoughts. We squeezed in a second visit to see Ludo just before Christmas. Between Christmas and New Year, we drove back to Northampton again to spend a couple of days with Rachel's family and meet up with old friends (including my friend Damo, who claims his grandma invented banoffee pie). Then on New Year's Eve, we went to collect Ludo.
Did Not Enter (Book Five in the DNF Series)

We drove home via a detour to meet up with my friend Damo (who claims his grandma invented Banoffee Pie) and his family, who were holidaying in Cornwall for a couple of weeks.
Did Not Happen (Book Six in the DNF Series)

We met up with my friend Damo (who claims his grandma invented banoffee pie), my sister and her family spent a couple of weeks down here in Devon, and Rachel's sister and family came down, too.

> Rachel's sister's family is currently undertaking an impressive challenge to climb the highest peaks in each county in England. Earlier in the year, we had joined them to climb Dunkery Hill, Somerset's highest peak. Then, during their holiday in Devon, we helped them tick off the highest peak in Devon – High Willhays (pronounced High Willies, which kept us all amused during the challenging walk).
> **Did Not Believe (Book Seven in the DNF Series)**

I am not sure if Damo ever read any of the *DNF Series*, but he certainly bought them all because I had another seven messages telling me I was a dick.

When I published *The Self-Help Bible*, I wondered whether it was time to bring the whole banoffee pie trend to an end. This book was a little different to the others and it felt like maybe it was time to close that chapter of my writing career.

As if! Of course I was going to mention it.

> Resolving conflict is an extremely tough challenge. I always want to be proved right and can be very stubborn. If I am proved right (which is 100% of the time, obvs) I do have a brief moment of extreme satisfaction. This passes quickly and is then outweighed by the guilt I feel on behalf of the other person. My friend Damo (who claims his grandma invented banoffee pie) is equally stubborn and we have had some intense, but healthy, arguments over the years. He once claimed you could pour an infinite amount of sugar into a cup of tea and it would dissolve away. The tea and sugar that spilled all over his parents' kitchen floor when I tried the experiment suggests he

was wrong.
The Self-Help Bible: All the Answers for a Happier, Healthier Life

I particularly like how this anecdote goes full-circle back to the kitchen table at Damo's parents' house, where the whole banoffee pie saga began.

In my last book, *Reconnecting...*, I managed to mention it in the very first sentence.

> My friend Mark and I were given the honour of being best men at the wedding of our friend Damo (who claims his grandma invented banoffee pie). One of our main duties was organising the stag do/bachelor party.
> ***Reconnecting: Tales of Adventure, Travel and Life***

And there we have it.

Seventeen books and 17 mentions of Damo claiming his grandma invented banoffee pie.

What began as an off-the-cuff reference in my first book has continued for the 12 years since its release. In those 12 years, I think I have had just two or three comments about Damo and his banoffee pie. I like that perhaps people don't even notice the references or just think they are a bit weird and gloss over them.

What is the truth? Did Damo's grandma really invent banoffee pie?

He denies ever claiming she did. Those of us who were there choose to remember what our beer-raddled minds heard at the time.

According to Wikipedia, banoffee pie was invented by Nigel Mackenzie and Ian Dowding at the Hungry Monk in East Sussex in the 1970s. There is no mention of Damo's grandma.

I sent Damo a message asking him to set the record straight. He replied:

> *I've known you for over 30 years and you finally ask what the real story is. lol. The banoffee pie was invented by the Hungry Monk restaurant in East Sussex. Someone my dad knew gave him a copy of the recipe. They lived in Sussex at the time. The recipe used a pie crust base. Everyone made it that way. My dad decided to make it with a biscuit base and it caught on.*

This real story is far more impressive than the one we have been incorrectly spreading for the last 30 years.

Damo's grandma did NOT invent banoffee pie.

His dad invented its biscuit base.

However, there is a plot twist.

Far from being the hero in this story, it turns out Damo's dad is the villain. Because Ian Dowding (one of the chefs credited with inventing banoffee pie) is quoted as saying that his 'pet hates are biscuit crumb bases and that horrible cream in aerosols'.

And that concludes the story of my friend Damo, and his dad, who ruined banoffee pie forever.

A Weekend in Cornwall with Storm Kathleen

With no plans for the school Easter holidays, I booked a last-minute long weekend for the family in a static caravan in Cornwall.

My 14-year-old soon, Leo, played in a football tournament on the Wednesday of that week and woke with a painful foot the following morning.

'I LITERALLY CAN'T WALK,' he declared while miraculously walking into the kitchen. 'MY FOOT IS DEFINITELY BROKEN!'

'Poor you,' I said, trying to sound as sympathetic as I could. 'Did you injure it at football yesterday?'

'I don't know. It seemed OK yesterday. But today it's the WORST PAIN I'VE EVER EXPERIENCED IN MY LIFE.'

Normally if someone declares this you should be quite concerned. But Leo is not known for having a high pain threshold and does have a history of debilitating injuries that come out of nowhere and then mysteriously disappear a few hours later.

'Well, just take it easy today and hopefully it will feel a bit better tomorrow,' I said.

He woke on the Friday morning – the day we were due to drive to Cornwall – and declared:

'IT'S TWICE AS BAD AS IT WAS YESTERDAY. IT IS GENUINELY 100% BROKEN!'

'Twice as bad as yesterday?' I asked. 'And yesterday was the worst pain you've ever experienced in your life?'

'YES! YOU DON'T UNDERSTAND! I NEED TO GO TO HOSPITAL. MY FOOT IS LITERALLY ABOUT TO FALL OFF.'

'Err... OK,' I said, still doing my best to play the role of sympathetic parent and not laugh at his histrionics.

Spending three days in Cornwall with Leo and his foot that was LITERALLY ABOUT TO FALL OFF didn't seem very fair on him, so we called into our local minor injuries unit on our way to Cornwall to get it looked at.

The minor injuries unit was closed.

So we drove for an hour and a half towards where we were staying for the weekend and stopped at the hospital in Bodmin instead. I dropped Rachel and Leo off, and then Layla, Kitty and I drove to a nearby supermarket to do a food shop for the weekend.

'There's an old, abandoned hospital near here,' said Layla (aged 16), on our way back. 'Maybe we should go and have a look.'

'How do you know?'

'I just googled *abandoned buildings in Bodmin*.'

'As you do,' said Kitty (aged 12). 'Layla, you're such a weirdo. Who googles stuff like that?'

'Oh be quiet, Kitty!' said Layla. 'Nobody asked you.'

'Alright, stop bickering. Where is this hospital?'

'It's three minutes this way. It looks amazing. St Lawrence's hospital – formerly called the County Lunatic Asylum.'

'Maybe we should leave you there, Layla!' cackled Kitty.

Layla didn't respond.

I followed Layla's directions, and we passed through an ornate gateway and then drove several laps around an upmarket housing estate, with no sign of any abandoned buildings, just lots of fancy houses, some of which looked like they were developed from the old hospital buildings.

'Er, when was the post you're reading written?'

'Oh,' said Layla. '2011.'

'Yeah, I think we are a bit late unfortunately,' I said.

'Great one, Layla!' said Kitty. 'That was a massive waste of time.'

'You're a massive waste of time,' said Layla.

We drove back to the hospital (the real one) and parked up. I read a text from Rachel saying Leo hadn't yet been seen by anyone.

I took Ludo for a walk around the hospital grounds and then got another message from Rachel to say they were waiting for an x-ray. Kitty and I took Ludo for another walk, and then I received the following two messages from Rachel:

Leo's foot is broken.

Is there room in the van for a wheelchair?

Oh my god. I felt so guilty for being so dismissive of Leo's claims of having a broken foot.

Rachel then sent another message.

Doctor said his foot is like a breadstick in a blender. (This is a quote from *This Country* when Kerry claims her foot has been smashed to smithereens playing football.)

I replied:

Oh no! Poor Leo. What happens now? Are they going to put it in a cast?

I returned to the car and told Layla the news. She and Kitty both looked like they too felt guilty for not being more sympathetic to Leo. I felt really awful. It turned out Leo didn't have a low pain threshold after all. He must have broken his foot during the football tournament and stoically played on with the injury. What sort of a parent was I for not taking his claims seriously?

Ten minutes later, Leo and Rachel emerged from the hospital doors into the car park. Leo was hobbling but there was no sign of a cast, crutches or a wheelchair.

It turns out Leo's foot wasn't broken. He had sent the message from Rachel's phone as a joke.

'So you lied?' said Layla. 'Your foot is fine?'

'No, it's not fine. It's honestly SO PAINFUL. It's probably WORSE THAN BROKEN.'

'But it's not broken?'

'No,' said Rachel. 'But it is very painful.'

'Leo, you are such an idiot,' said Kitty.

The x-ray had come back clear. He had instead been diagnosed with sesamoiditis. I had never heard of sesamoiditis but googled it and it sounds exactly like what Leo was experiencing (an inflammation of the bones and tendons in the ball of the foot) and also very painful. The fact that Leo – aged 14 – has grown several inches in the last few weeks presumably has something to do with it too. I was noticeably taller than him at Christmas and he's now significantly taller than me. Or maybe I've shrunk.

I think Leo was almost disappointed his foot wasn't broken as that would have given validation for the amount of pain he was in. Rachel and I tried to reassure him that it didn't have to be broken for us to believe he was in pain. We told him he could take it easy for the weekend and didn't have to do anything he didn't want to do.

Storm Kathleen was due to hit the UK during our weekend holiday. Three nights in a static caravan perched on an exposed hillside on the north coast of Cornwall during torrential rain and 65mph wind was not ideal, but we were looking forward to the short break.

The sleepy village of Crantock sits next to the Gannel Estuary, on the opposite bank to the busy seaside town of Newquay. We had stayed in Newquay twice in the last few years, and loved this quieter western side, so thought it would be a good place to base ourselves for a weekend.

I suggested to the children that they each bring a book with them, in case of the horrific event of there being no Wi-Fi or phone signal at the site. I discovered, while unpacking the car, that Leo's book of choice was the dictionary.

'I just grabbed the biggest book I could see on the shelf,' was his justification. Fortunately for him, the site did have Wi-Fi, and, unsurprisingly, Leo's dictionary didn't get much of a look-in during the weekend.

Our static caravan in Crantock was a five-minute walk down the hill to the beach. After unloading the car, we left Leo and his dictionary and headed out to explore. We climbed the sand dunes and then Rachel and I had a quick swim from the river beach of the estuary, before returning to the caravan for pizza and *Daddy's Home 2* (one of our favourite films – despite its grossly unfair 21% rating on Rotten Tomatoes), while the rain and wind battered the caravan from all sides.

Five people and a dog in one caravan is quite crowded, so we spent as much time outside as possible during the weekend. Storm Kathleen was doing her best to put us off, but we weren't going to be kept inside. I managed four swims from the estuary beach during our three-night stay, one on the first evening and a pre-breakfast dip each morning. We played two rounds of crazy golf on the Saturday (yes, I dominated!) and Ludo had four walks.

He was so tired that he didn't even notice when Rachel accidentally threw her coat on him.

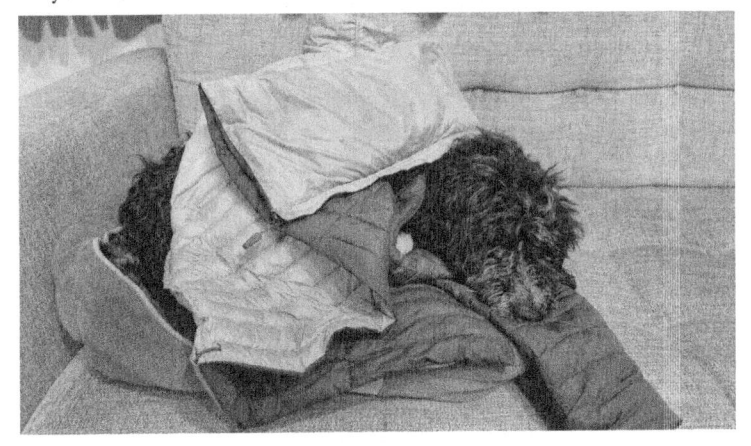

Catherine, one of Rachel's closest friends from university, was walking the South West Coast Path and coincidentally passing through Crantock during our stay. Rather than join her for some of her walk and then have to double-back the way we came, we thought it would make more sense to leave our van further along the coast so that we could join her for a longer one-way walk.

On the Saturday evening, Rachel and I drove to Perranporth, parked the van on a side street just outside town, and then ran home. We opted for the more direct, six-mile road route, rather than following the longer and more challenging coast path. It was a wise decision as if we had known what lay in store for us, we might have had second thoughts about doing the walk the following day.

This had happened on a previous holiday in Newquay a couple of years ago. Rachel and I drove and parked the van near to Bedruthen Steps, and then ran the six miles back along the coast to the holiday park where we were staying, with the aim of then walking back to the van with Layla, Leo and Kitty later that day. However, Rachel decided that it was too windy, the coast path too steep, and the cliffs too precipitous for us to take the dog and children, so I ended up having to run the six miles back to the van later that day on my own.

Leo's foot was still very sore on the Sunday morning so he wasn't going to be joining us for the walk to Perranporth. Layla's original plan had been to stay in the caravan and do some of her art, but given the choice of a gruelling walk along the coast in severe gale-force winds or a day in the caravan with her brother, she opted for the walk.

We met Catherine in the beach car park at about 11 am in breezy but dry conditions. The forecast was for severe wind and intermittent showers all day.

It had been a few years since we had seen Catherine, and it was lovely to catch up and hear about her South West Coast Path adventure so far. Starting in Minehead, she had walked the nearly 200 miles along the coast of Somerset, Devon and Cornwall to Crantock, camping some nights and staying in youth hostels on others. Her plan was to continue to Land's End (another 60+ miles) before resuming the second half of the walk later in the year.

We traversed the sand dunes around Crantock Beach and then around the headland of Pentire Point to the beautiful beach of Porth Joke (known locally as Polly Joke, which is derived from the Cornish Pol-Lejouack, meaning Jackdaw Cove).

A colony of seals have made their home in one of the coves between Porth Joke and Kelsey Head and we stood and watched them from high above on the coast path. These were the first seals Catherine had seen in her 200-mile walk.

As we crested the headland at Kelsey Head, we felt the full force of the wind. I was recording a video when Catherine's waterproof rucksack cover blew off and cartwheeled across the headland. Kitty instinctively raced after it. Catherine tried to go and help but then let go of her visor, which also blew away. I eventually stopped laughing and filming and ran off to try to help. By the time I got over the top of the hill, Kitty was nowhere to be seen. She eventually appeared clutching the orange rucksack cover. It had blown all the way over the peninsula near to where we had stood and watched the seals, and she trudged back up the hill looking utterly exhausted, but triumphant that she had successfully completed her mission.

We had walked a loop from Crantock while staying in Newquay last year along the coast to Holywell Bay, and it wasn't until we arrived at Holywell that I remembered Leo's mysterious foot injury that had plagued him during our previous visit. His foot had been so painful during that walk (LITERALLY BROKEN, if I remember correctly) that he, Rachel and Kitty ended up getting a bus back to Newquay from Holywell and Layla, Ludo and I walked back to pick up the van from Crantock.

It seems Leo's debilitating injuries have a habit of surfacing when there is a long walk on the cards. Purely coincidental, I'm sure.

Holywell Bay is a spectacular white-sandy beach backed by dramatic sand dunes with rocky outcrops out to sea. We trudged up and over the dunes and then across the beach, sandblasted in our faces the entire way. From Holywell, we followed the coast path up around the edge of Penhale Camp – an abandoned military camp, built in the Second World War, and left unoccupied for over ten years.

We met another walker who had been heading the same way as us and she had been forced to turn back because the wind was so strong. We didn't really have any choice but to keep going as our van was parked another five miles into the wind.

Seconds after dismissing the woman's claims about the wind, an almighty gust took Rachel's legs from underneath her and she fell flat on her front. Catherine and Kitty were also taken down too, although we are not sure if it was the wind or Rachel that wiped them out.

I don't think I have ever experienced wind like it. Thankfully, there was a wooden fence for us to cling onto as we persevered around the exposed promontory.

Walking the perimeter of Penhale Camp was an eerie experience. It is currently the subject of an ongoing planning dispute, with proposals to turn it into a holiday park. The site still has 97 buildings and would once have been a constant hive of activity when in use. The only noise now was the deafening roar of the wind. A high fence topped with razor wire borders the site, with signs warning of risks of explosions. Even Layla, with her desire to explore abandoned buildings, looked like she would rather be anywhere else.

We were caught between not wanting to walk on the coast path, because of a fear of being blown over the edge and tumbling to our deaths, and not wanting to walk off the coast path because of a fear of being blown up.

Adjacent to Penhale Camp sits Count House. One of the most dramatic houses I have ever seen which looked like some sort of CGI or AI generated image. A chilling, deserted military camp to one side of it, and dramatic cliffs to the other. It was up for sale last year (for £2.5 million) but there is no sign of anyone living there at the moment.

Layla and Kitty had both had enough by this point and were understandably ready for the walk to be over. Ludo kept looking at me as if to say, 'Are we really still going?' I kept alternating between putting him on and off his lead, wanting to hold onto him in case a gust of wind blew him away, and not wanting him to trip me up and send me over the edge.

We then rounded a corner and saw Perranporth Beach laid out in front of us. Laying eyes on Perranporth – the end point of our walk – should have been a momentous occasion.

'Hooray, we can finally see Perranporth!' I said, trying to sound optimistic.

'Where?' said Kitty.

'There!' I said, pointing into the distance.

'You've got to be joking,' said Layla.

Unfortunately, Perranporth Beach is about three miles long and the end still looked demoralisingly far away. There were a few tears from certain members of our group at this point, but we knew there was no choice but to battle on.

Rather than following the coast path through the dunes, battling the ups and downs in a severe sandstorm, we chose to head down onto the beach and cover as much of the distance as possible on the firmer sand.

At the northern end of the beach, we found a small cave and tropical pool, with a couple of gated tunnel entrances – one open and one closed. When we googled it later, we found this pool is part of Gravel Hill Mine (formerly Penhale Iron Mine) and that the pool was the entrance to hundreds of feet of old mining tunnels. Rachel and I had been tempted to have a swim, but after watching a YouTube video of the deep, dark and extremely ominous shafts below, we were very glad we didn't.

It was a long slog along Perranporth Beach, our faces all red and burnt from the wind and sand, but I think it would have been preferable to the path through the dunes.

Towards the southern end of the beach, we followed the concrete path that zigzags up the side of the cliff, back to the South West Coast Path, and if we had left it any later, the tide would have cut us off from this access point and it would have been a much more challenging ascent up the sandy cliff.

There were plenty of other positives from the day too. The scenery was stunning. We are slowly ticking off sections of the South West Coast Path, and each new section fills me with awe and delight.

It had stayed dry! The predicted rain hadn't arrived, and it would have been unbearably miserable battling rain as well as the wind. I love extreme wind like that and it's a wonderful reminder of the power of nature.

I had told Layla and Kitty the walk would be about seven miles. As usual, I had underestimated. By the time we finally reached Perranporth we had covered ten miles, all of them on steep or sandy terrain into a fierce headwind. But Layla and Kitty had both done brilliantly, and despite plenty of miserable moments, I think they were both proud to have completed it. Not that they will ever admit it.

The promise of looking around the shops in Perranporth had been part of the motivation for Layla and Kitty to do the walk in the first place, but by the time we arrived, neither of them had any desire to take another step. So Rachel bought ice creams and snacks from the closest shop while I walked up the final hill to get the van. I did have a brief moment of panic when I couldn't find the car key, but thankfully located it buried in my rucksack.

Catherine said it had been the toughest leg of her journey so far. I think she enjoyed having company for the day and we loved experiencing a small part of her challenge with her. It was 4 pm when we left Catherine in Perranporth and she decided she didn't want to walk any further either, so checked into a campsite for an early night.

We drove back to the caravan and Leo was still lying on the sofa bed where we left him, with an empty Pot Noodle and a half-drunk glass of coke next to the bed.

'How was your day?' he said, yawning.

'It was great,' I said. 'Pretty eventful, but really good fun. How was your day?'

'I'm SO TIRED,' he said. 'I've LITERALLY never been more EXHAUSTED.'

Layla and Kitty both glared at him.

'TIRED?' snapped Layla. 'You have no idea!'

THE TESCO CAR PARK MARATHON

A FEW MONTHS BACK, my friend Tim suggested running a marathon around the car park of our local Tesco.

Why? I am still unsure.

'That sounds like a really, really stupid idea,' I said. 'But I'd probably be up for giving it a go at some point.'

Out of curiosity, I walked a lap of the car park to gauge the distance using my watch. One lap was 0.12 miles. A marathon would be 218 laps. It's a fairly small car park and, initially, that number didn't sound too intimidating.

My wife Rachel and I have been running a marathon every month since January 2020, sometimes together, sometimes separately. Most of our routes are scenic coastal trails, so the idea of 218 laps of Tesco car park wasn't exactly enticing.

Last Sunday was the London Marathon – a race I participated in back in 2009 (my first ever marathon) and I have applied and been rejected every year since. Rachel secured a place again this year (her third) by qualifying with a good-for-age time.

Since Rachel received her acceptance email and I received yet another rejection last July, London Marathon chatter has been incessant. Admittedly, I found myself zoning out whenever Rachel brought it up. Perhaps it was a childish reaction born out of jealousy. Every time she mentioned it, it felt like she was saying *'Did you know I'm running the London Marathon and you're not?'* We debated all going up for the weekend to support her, but costs and logistics meant just Rachel and Layla made the trip.

Leo had a football match on Sunday and we got home just in time to turn on the TV and watch Rachel cross the finish line in a very impressive three hours and 37 minutes – her second fastest ever.

With my April marathon still to do, I asked Tim if he fancied attempting the Tesco car park marathon on the same day. Tim agreed but somehow managed to turn it around and imply I was the one suggesting something ludicrous.

'It was your stupid idea in the first place,' I reminded him.

'Yes, but I didn't think we would actually do it.'

It seemed oddly fitting – a stark contrast to the grandeur of the London Marathon with its 50,000 runners, throngs of spectators, and millions watching from home. While the London course boasts iconic landmarks like Tower Bridge, St Paul's Cathedral, the Palace of Westminster and Buckingham Palace, our marathon would feature two blokes circling an empty car park, with no spectators in sight – just a battle of wills against our own minds.

Running laps around the car park during opening hours was out of the question, given the chaos of cars, trolleys and shoppers (although having obstacles might have added a fun dynamic to it). Sunday evening was ideal, with the supermarket closing at 4pm.

I met Tim just after 5pm. To my surprise, he had crafted race numbers for both of us, adding a touch of legitimacy to our completely pointless endeavour.

The car park at Tesco has a camera-controlled two-hour limit, so we couldn't even park our own cars in it while we ran. Instead, we left them in a neighbouring pay-and-display, and each took a bag of supplies with us down to Tesco's car park – our makeshift running track.

One of the benefits (who am I kidding? The ONLY benefit) of running multiple small laps, is that we didn't have to carry anything with us. Almost all of the marathons I run these days are self-supported and require me to haul around a backpack full of food and water.

We each left a bag of supplies (mine contained three bottles of water, cheese sandwiches, crisps, bananas and apples) against the wall on the far side of the car park. I briefly considered laying out some snacks along the curb, but a curious seagull quickly put an end to that idea.

'Do we just start?' I asked.

'I guess so,' said Tim. 'Which way do we go?'

'I suppose we should follow the arrows. It's like they've marked the course out for us already.'

The first few laps were quite enjoyable. The car park was perfectly flat and those 218 laps would disappear in no time.

The realisation of the stupidity of what we were undertaking hit us midway through lap nine. It felt like we had been running for a while and were making good progress. And then my watch beeped to tell me we had completed our first mile. Over eight laps in and we were still 25.2 miles (210 laps) from finishing. It was going to be a very long evening. That initial novelty of the challenge had quickly given way to sheer tedium.

After about 15 minutes, a friend of ours and his wife arrived to use one of the electric car-charging stations. They were there for 20 minutes, and we chatted briefly each time we passed. Strangely, they didn't once question why we were running laps of a supermarket car park.

After an hour (about 50 laps) we tried reversing the loop and running in the opposite direction. For some reason it was much harder anti-clockwise. We were now running against the arrows of the one-way system, and it was almost as though we were fighting against some physical resistance. Perhaps it was also because it felt a little like we were undoing all the hard work we had done when running clockwise. I almost expected the distance on my watch to start decreasing.

We struggled through another 50 laps 'against the current' and then reverted to the correct, current-assisted direction for the remainder.

MAKE FUNNY

As the hours dragged on, we grew increasingly tired and hungry. The fully stocked supermarket teased us every minute or two as we passed, its shelves laden with any food you could dream of – the ultimate aid station. If only it had been open.

Tim has a history of things going wrong for him during sporting challenges. We took part in an iron-distance triathlon together (see *Did Not Believe*) and he dropped his bike during transition and only had five gears for the hilly 112-mile bike leg. The night before the triathlon, his hydration pack sprung a leak for no apparent reason and then his bike got a flat tyre while stored inside his van. Several times I have met him for a run or bike ride and a crucial bit of his kit has either been missing or broken. Every marathon I have ever run with him he has stopped his watch too early or forgotten to un-pause it, so he has a series of not-quite full distance marathons recorded.

It didn't seem possible that he would be able to have any sort of mishap during our Tesco car park marathon. Surely he was safe within the confines of our 0.12-mile bubble.

Two hours into our run, Tim spotted a parking attendant patrolling the neighbouring car park.

'I'd better just check to make sure my parking payment went through,' he joked, pulling out his phone to check the parking app.

As he unlocked his phone, there was a loading screen and then a *'payment confirmed'* notification popped up. It seemed he had inadvertently locked his phone before the payment had been fully processed.

'Shit, I'd better go and check he's not giving me a ticket.'

He ran off up the hill to the other car park and I stood and ate a banana, checked the football scores and laughed at Tim's latest misfortune.

He returned ten minutes later holding a parking ticket.

'I was too late,' he sighed. 'It was already 'in the system' apparently.'

'Did you tell him you had tried to pay via the app?'

'Yes, he told me to appeal it and they might let me off.'

'Did you tell him you were running a marathon?'

'Yes, he asked me when it was going to start, and I told him we were already halfway through. He said, 'Oh, sorry for interrupting'.'

'Ha, I love that you got a ticket for parking in a car park that we parked in specifically so that we didn't get a parking ticket.'

The parking ticket incident was a nice little interlude to the tedium of the run.

We had another break from the monotony for 20 minutes when I put the radio on via my phone and we listened to the end of the FA Cup semi-final between Manchester United and Coventry City, when Coventry came back from 3-0 down to force extra time. Coventry then scored in the final minutes of extra time, only for the goal to be disallowed after a controversial VAR decision. Manchester United scraped through as winners in the penalty shootout. I am only mentioning this because those 20 minutes were the most enjoyable of the entire run.

The constant corners prevented us from settling into a rhythm, making the entire experience uncomfortable and unpleasant. I am used to slow, hilly, off-road marathons, which involve a lot of walking, and I was not prepared for the pace and monotony of running laps around a flat car park.

The scenery became a repetitive blur of painted lines and parking bays. The whole experience was anything but exhilarating.

The distance on our watches was going up so slowly. We noticed the seconds, the minutes, the hours tick by as our required distance of 26.22 miles still seemed like an insurmountable way off. We began to question whether there were GPS issues, with the signal being confused by us running is such small circles. Perhaps we had actually run much further than our watches had recorded? That was wishful thinking. We were just getting slower and slower.

We longed for some scenery – the fields, the lanes, the beaches that we are lucky enough to live within running distance of. Even some hills would have been preferable to that same 0.12-mile loop of Tesco car park.

'Yay!' I said, after three-and-a-bit hours. 'Just 10km to go!'

'Woohoo!' said Tim, sarcastically. 'That's 50 more laps.'

'Oh god, that sounds so depressing.'

There was a temptation to leave the confines of the car park and complete the remaining distance on a more interesting and less repetitive loop. But then it would have felt like we had failed. We had set out to run a marathon around Tesco car park and anything other than that would have been unacceptable.

Running a marathon late in the day had the added disadvantage of meaning we already had a day's worth of activity before it began. I had been on two dog walks, been linesman for Leo's football match and had completed 16,000 steps before we even started. I topped 60,000 by the end of the day.

We were both suffering from tightness and cramps in our legs, hips and shoulders. I had read somewhere that running backwards for a short distance can help loosen up muscles.

So, we both gave it a try.

'Actually, I think this is a bad idea,' I said. 'I just had a premonition of waking up in a hospital bed and you telling me I'd tripped over and knocked myself unconscious with five laps to go.'

'Well, if that happened, I would call an ambulance, drag you into one of the parking bays, and then finish my remaining laps while I waited for the ambulance.'

'Thanks, that's good to know. I would do exactly the same for you.'

It was surprisingly easy to fill those hours with chat. A lot of it was about the tedium of running around a car park, but we did our best to distract ourselves from the monotony as much as possible. I don't think I would have been able to do it on my own. Perhaps running such a boring marathon solo you might be able to get into some sort of deep meditative state. But I think it's more likely I would have given up after five laps and gone home.

We laughed regularly at the absurdity of it all. Since Tim suggested the Tesco car park marathon a few months ago I had thought about it regularly and wondered what it would be like. And now I've found out. And I know that I never want to do it again.

My watch eventually ticked over to 26.22 miles after four hours and 16 minutes of running. I joined Tim for another half a lap until his watch did the same.

Tesco Car Park Marathon

Distance	Avg Pace
26.23 mi	9:46 /mi

Moving Time	Elevation Gain
4:16:08	728 ft

After dropping the children at school the following morning, I called into Tesco as I do several times a week. The car park felt strangely different, now forever imprinted with the memories of our meaningless challenge.

Running a marathon in an empty supermarket car park may not have been the most glamorous or thrilling experience, but it was an adventure, nonetheless. One that tested our endurance, resilience and sanity in a unique way. I felt a sense of pride in what we had accomplished. We had somehow achieved a small victory in the most unexpected of places.

A friend of mine suggested the Tesco Car Park Marathon should become an annual event for those of us who fail to get a place in the London Marathon. With this in mind, I have entered the ballot for London next year and have my fingers tightly crossed for an outcome that spares me having to do another lap around that bloody car park.

The Cat Next Door

The Story of D2, the Coolest Cat in the World

When our neighbours moved back to England after 15 years living in Spain, they brought with them an astonishing 17 dogs and 33 cats. In Spain, they ran an animal refuge for strays, and when they returned, so did their menagerie.

The dogs are an eclectic bunch, coming in all shapes and sizes, with not a recognisable breed among them. Some of them don't even look like dogs.

The cats are a little different. Regardless of their breed, most of them are, well, cat-sized and look... er... cat-like.

Given their backgrounds as former strays, most of the cats were quite nervous and wary of humans to begin with. They would scatter at the sight of us, preferring to keep their distance. So, it was a surprise when one day, after returning from school pickup, I found a large, fluffy ginger cat sitting nonchalantly on one of the children's skateboards outside our house.

'Who the hell is this guy?' I wondered.

I took a photo from the driver's seat and posted it to my Facebook page. Little did I know, this would be the start of a delightful photographic journey with the coolest cat I've ever known.

> **George Mahood**
> 10 Nov 2019
>
> The cat next door is cool as fuck.
>
> 639 — 41 comments • 3 shares

The cat is called D2. He was found living outside a hairdresser's in Malaga. The salon owner named him after another stray cat they'd called Dave. When this one appeared, he became 'Dave 2', later shortened to D2.

Most of the cats that returned from Spain now live inside and have become fairly domesticated house cats. However, some, like D2, are so used to outdoor life and remain a bit wary of humans (and the 17 dogs they would be sharing a house with) that they choose to stay outside, sleeping in the farm buildings and being fed outdoors instead.

For the first few years, D2 was a little wary of us. Despite his apparent arrogance, he would skulk away if approached. One day, it struck me that he was Spanish. I greeted him, 'Hola D2. ¿Qué tal?' and from then on, he seemed to gradually warm to us.

Our dog Ludo and the farm dog Tan sometimes chase the other cats if they spot them. But Ludo and Tan never mess with D2.

He is untouchable. He has an aura of unflappable coolness that commands respect from everyone.

I recently started taking our other neighbour's dog Milo on walks with us, and he was introduced to D2 for the first time. Milo bounded towards D2 enthusiastically, D2 hissed, warning Milo that he would tear his face off (in Spanish, of course, but Milo got the message) and Milo has stayed away from him ever since.

D2 is often found sitting in the middle of the farmyard and is unfazed by cars and tractors, which all have to manoeuvre around him. Rachel and I will often have to do an ambitious 15-point turn when we're trying to leave the house because he's sunbathing in a particular spot in the driveway.

This is a collection of some of the photos I have taken of D2 over the years, and the assortment of places he chooses to sit. The skateboard photo was taken in November 2019 and the most recent – him sitting on a stack of post mix concrete – was taken this morning (May, 2024).

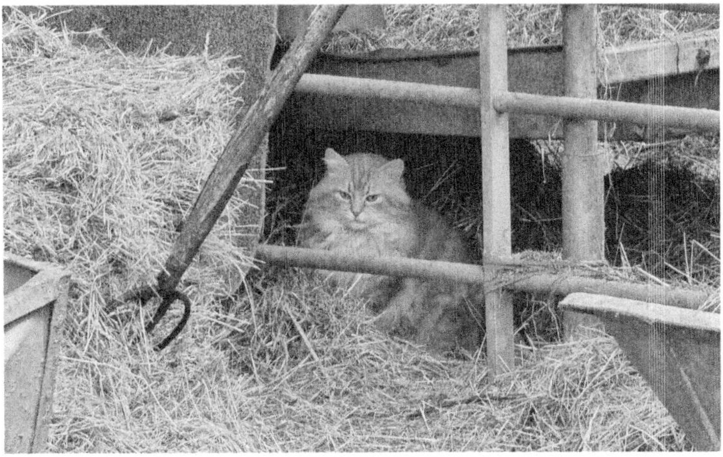

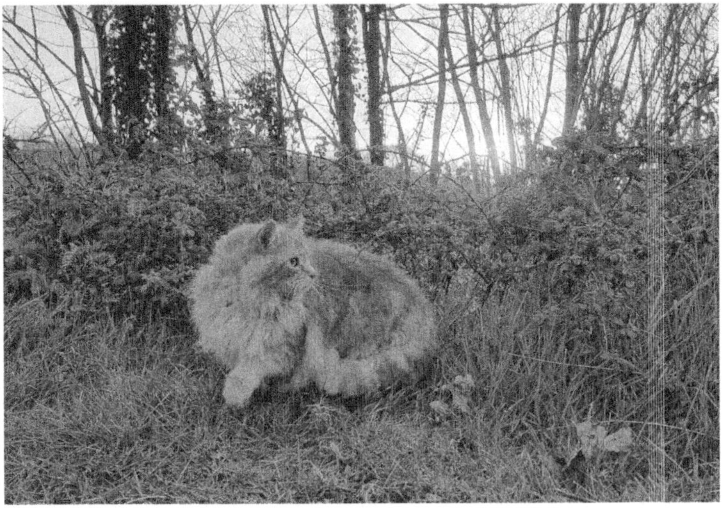

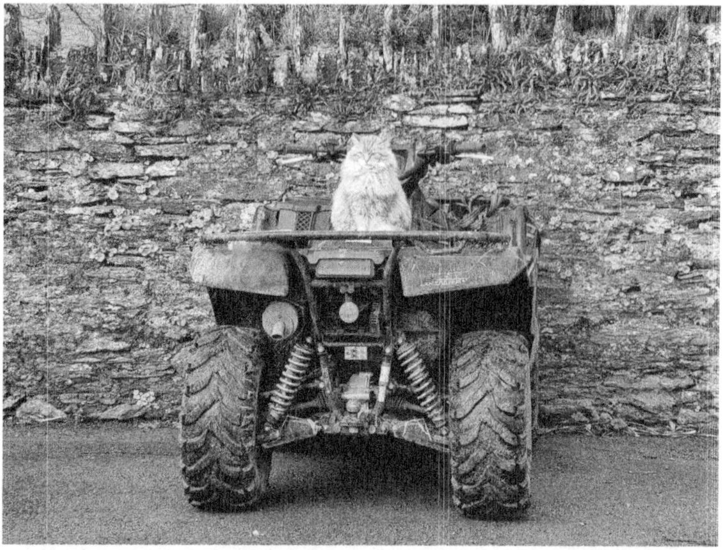

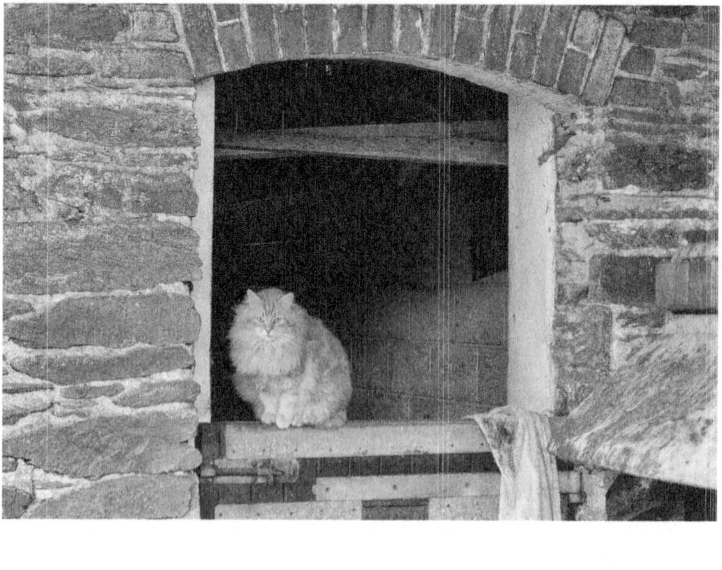

MAKE FUNNY

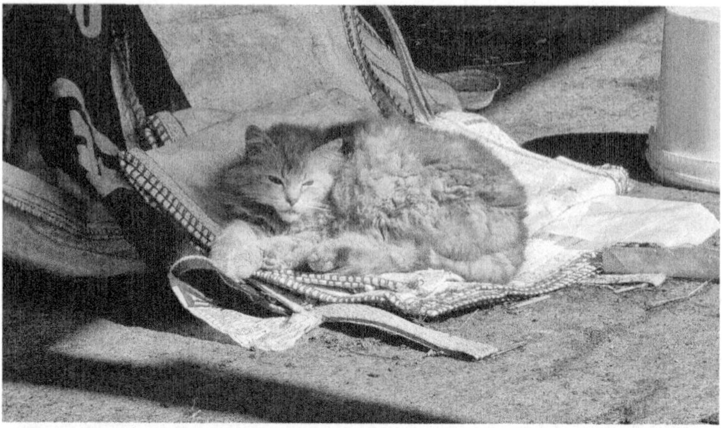

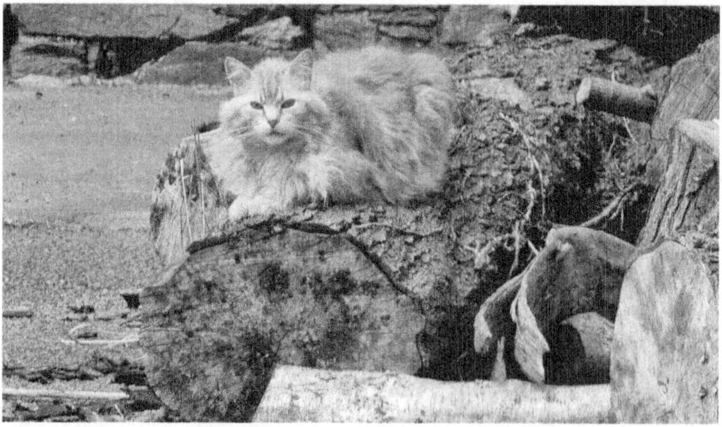

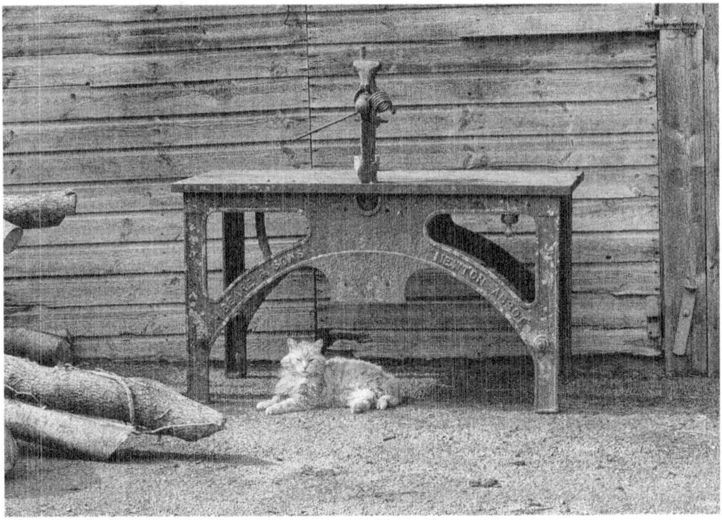

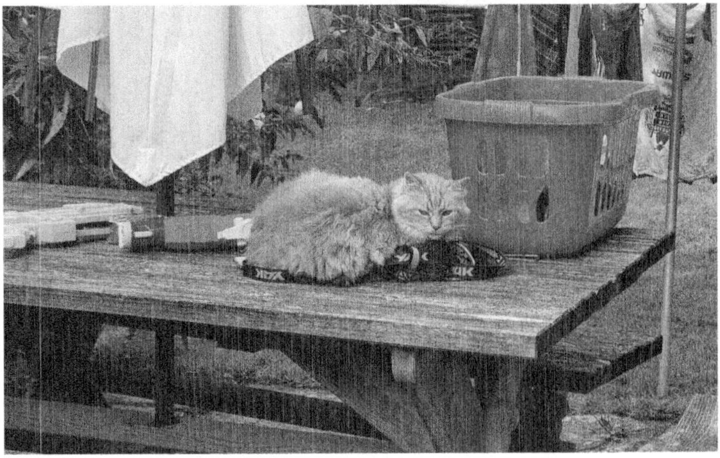

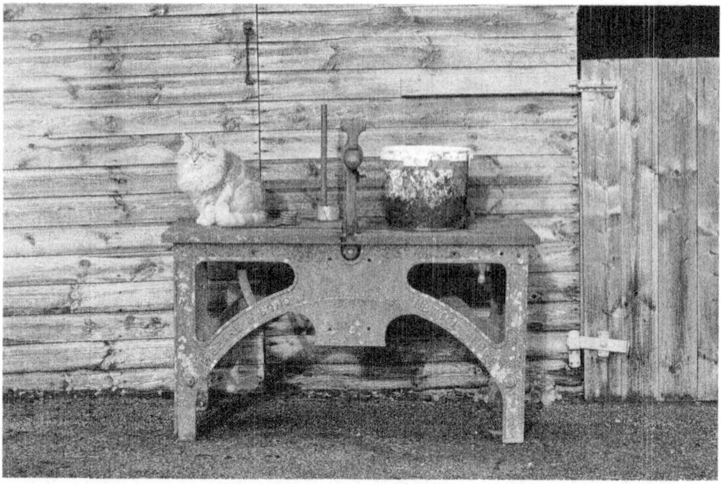

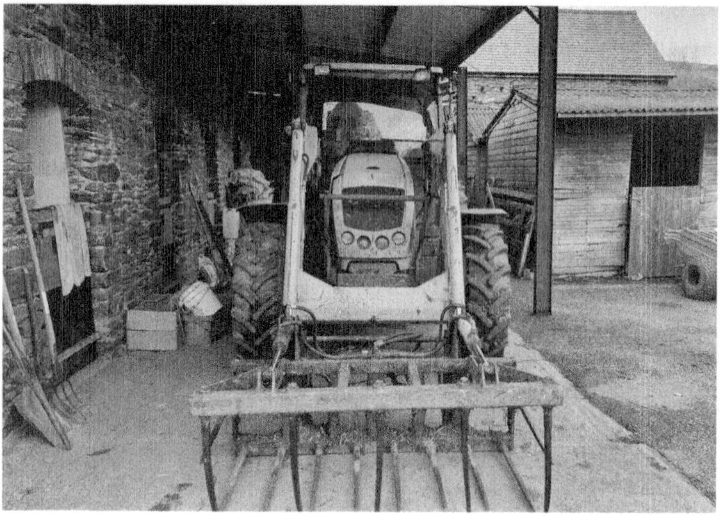

MAKE FUNNY

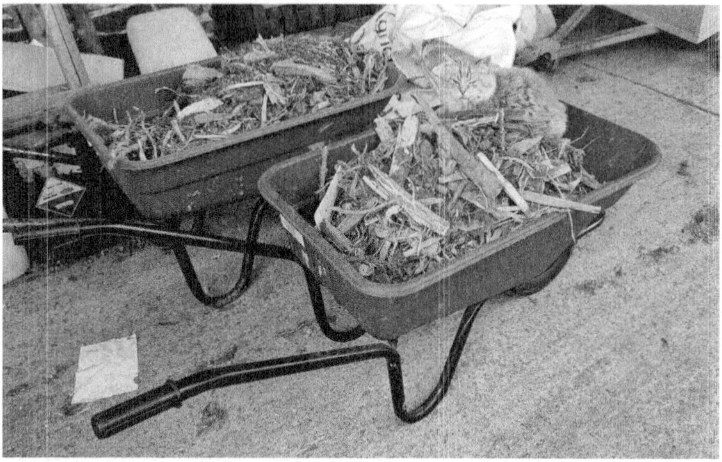

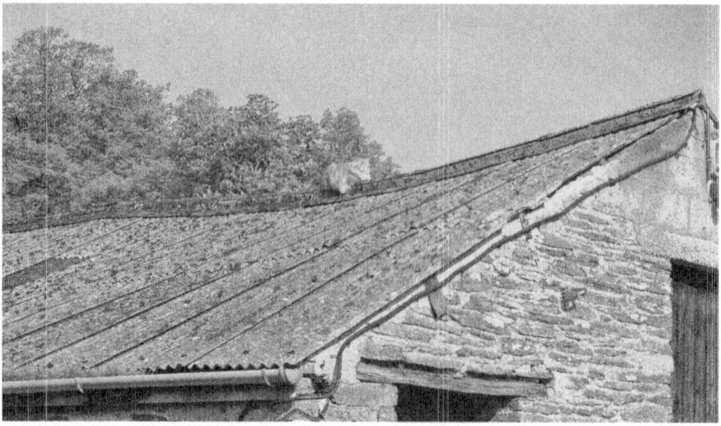

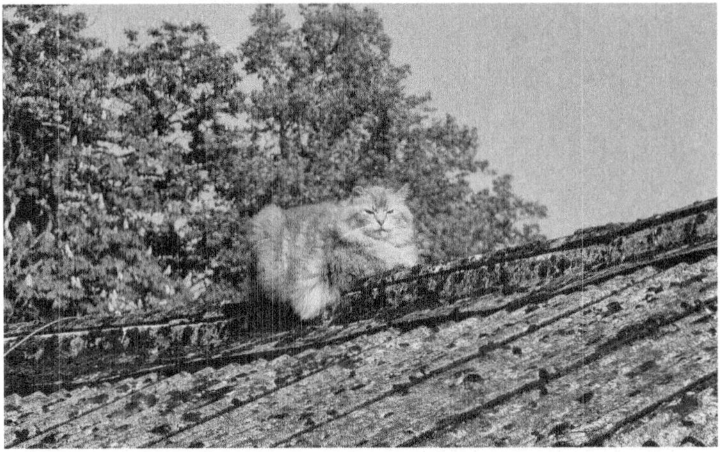

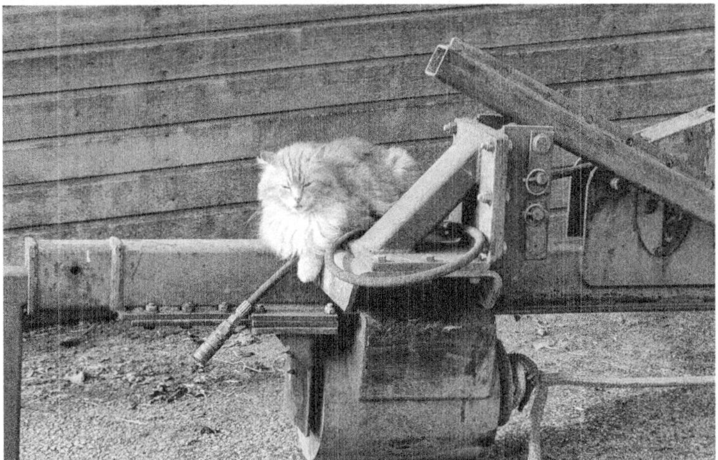

Layla has grown particularly fond of D2 and is hoping that one day he might decide to become a house cat. Our house cat. Last week, we found D2 at our front door, following a trail of cat treats that Layla had laid. She's trying to persuade the rest of us that D2 moving in to our house is a good idea. I opened my birthday present from Layla a few weeks ago and found she had drawn and framed me this picture.

But let's be honest, D2 will never become a house cat. Why would he when he's already the king of the farm? He's got the whole place wrapped around his little paw. Instead, we'll continue to admire him in his natural domain, the undisputed coolest cat in the world.

A Jog in a Bog

A Dartmoor running adventure

For my birthday last year, Rachel surprised me with a voucher for a night at the Two Bridges Hotel on Dartmoor. Like many vouchers, it ended up forgotten, buried in the back of a cupboard. As my birthday approached this year, we rediscovered the voucher, only to find out it was expiring within a week.

'What about this Friday?' suggested Rachel.

'Sounds good to me,' I said.

So last Friday, Rachel and I dropped Layla, Leo and Kitty at school, and set off for the Two Bridges Hotel.

We initially planned for a leisurely day with a short walk and a pub lunch, but the conversation took a predictable turn when Rachel suggested running a marathon instead.

'Really? It was only two weeks ago since we did our last one. And it's only May 2nd.'

'I know, that means you get the rest of the month to relax.'

'Fine,' I sighed.

I am not going to bore you with tales of all my monthly marathons, but this particular one deserves a writeup.

Rachel had found a route online for a 20-mile off-road loop that started and ended in Princetown, which was about 1.5 miles from our hotel. Running to and from the start of the loop would take us to 23 miles and we could add whatever additional mileage was needed at the end to take it up to 26.2 miles.

We parked our van in the hotel's car park and called into reception.

'We've got a room booked for tonight,' said Rachel. 'Is it OK if we leave our car in the car park while we go for a run?'

'Of course. Check in is at 3pm, but if your room is available earlier you can check in then.'

'Thank you,' I said. 'But I think it is very unlikely that we will be finished before 3pm.'

She glanced at her watch (it was 10am) and looked very confused. I could tell she was thinking, *What sort of a run takes more than five hours?*

The road climbs steeply from Two Bridges towards Princetown – the highest and largest settlement on Dartmoor – with views of Dartmoor Prison to our right.

We reached Princetown and turned left onto a gravel bridleway which stretched ahead of us onto the moor. I naively thought that this nicely surfaced, well-marked trail might continue for the entirety of our route. Oh, how wrong I could be.

Three miles into our run, we encountered Siward's Cross, a stone monument dating back to the 11th century. It marks the junction of the Monk's Path and the Abbots' Way – two of the main tracks across the moor – that historically linked the abbeys in Tavistock, Buckland and Buckfast.

Buckfast Abbey is famous for its Buckfast Tonic – a fortified wine with added caffeine that has weirdly become very popular in Scotland – and I wonder if this drink played a part in the willingness of the monks to trek across the moor.

Just below Siward's Cross lies the striking Nun's Cross Farm. Built in 1870 by John Hooper and his wife, it is surely one of the most remote houses in the UK.

The farm is the subject of many folklore tales and ghost stories, including an often-recounted one of a farmer's wife heading out to check on the cows in the middle of the night and never returning.

I have converted these photos to black and white to make them look more ghostly and sinister. It was actually fairly bright and sunny when we visited, and the house looked like a wonderful spot for a holiday. You can hire the place out and Rachel got excited about the idea of getting a big group of friends together and spending a few days there. There was a young family in the doorway, packing all their stuff away and we asked them what it had been like to stay at Nun's Cross.

'It's been quite an experience,' said the man. 'You're welcome to come and have a look around.'

So, we did. The house has a basic kitchen and sitting area, with three bedrooms that accommodate up to 27 people in seriously uncomfortable-looking wire bunk beds.

The romance of staying there quickly wore off.

The couple and their very young child had brought all their own food, bedding and firewood for five days. And with no access for vehicles, it had involved a 3-mile walk along a rutted track pushing a wheelbarrow.

'On second thoughts,' said Rachel, after we had said goodbye to the young family, 'I think I much prefer the sound of our hotel.'

We continued east, directly across the open moor. The terrain looked harmless enough, but it was getting a lot more challenging underfoot. What began as the occasional patch of marshy ground, quickly became bog in all directions, intersected with tussocks of grass. There was no longer any evidence of a path, and we were right in the middle of one of Dartmoor's many mires.

My watch told me we were now officially 'off-course' from the route we were supposed to be following. As if we had needed that confirmed.

Arthur Conan Doyle wrote about Dartmoor's mires in *The Hound of the Baskervilles*:

> 'A false step yonder means death to man or beast. Only yesterday I saw one of the moor ponies wander into it. He never came out. I saw his head for quite a long time craning out of the bog-hole, but it sucked him down at last. Even in dry seasons it is a danger to cross it, but after these autumn rains it is an awful place. And yet I can find my way to the very heart of it and return alive.'

We seemed to have found our way into the very heart of it. Now we just needed to return alive.

I heard another tale (apocryphal, I hope) of Dartmoor and its mires:

While out walking one day, a woman stumbled upon a hat lying in a patch of mud on the ground. She picked it up and beneath the hat was a man. And beneath the man was his horse.

It was impossible to do any sort of running. It was impossible to even walk. Trying to keep our feet dry was futile as we picked our way from tussock to tussock.

Rachel fell over four times in the space of 20 minutes. Thankfully the landings were very soft, and she remained uninjured. Each time she fell, I did the right thing and took a photo before offering to help her up.

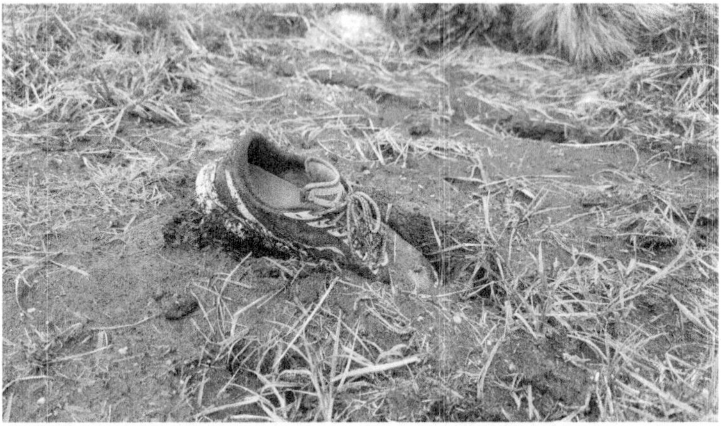

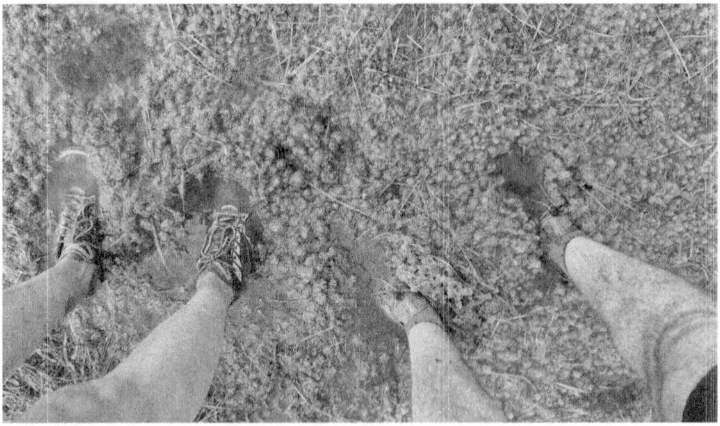

On one occasion, I took out my phone to take a photo of the scenery. Rachel stumbled next to me, lunged and grabbed my arm to steady herself, knocking my phone from my hand. Somehow, I caught it midair as it cartwheeled towards the bog.

My watch eventually beeped to tell us we were back 'on-course'. Yet we were still wading knee-deep in a swamp. It seemed the person whose route we were following had also followed this route through the mire. Or perhaps this was the only way.

I thought back to those monks who used to make this trek across the moor all those centuries ago, in their long robes and impractical shoes. That Buckfast Tonic must have been bloody good.

I took one small tumble but mostly managed to stay upright. My time would come spectacularly a little later.

I knew Dartmoor was an unforgiving place. But this experience gave me a whole new level of respect for the moor. Navigating proved challenging, even with GPS guidance. We had found ourselves off-course, stranded in the wilderness with no one but the bog for company. If the weather had turned or one of us had been injured, it would've been a different story altogether.

We passed a couple of wooden posts standing in the middle of the open moor. Each had a metal bracket on the top with instructions of where to place your camera and which direction to take the photo.

We had not seen another person in over an hour, and it seemed absurd that Dartmoor National Park would waste the time, effort and money to erect selfie posts in the middle of nowhere. Especially as the view we were looking at wasn't even that special. There were no rocky tors, rivers or interesting geographical features. Just bleak open moorland. Still, we thought we would make use of the posts, so I propped up my phone and set up a self-timer.

'Back a bit,' I said to Rachel.

'Here?'

'No, left a bit. Stand on that tuft of grass.'

'This one?'

'No, back a bit. The next one. Just beyond that patch of mud. Yes, that's it. Stay there. Five...four...three...'

The wind blew my phone over on the first two attempts, but we succeeded on my third.

It wasn't until I went to retrieve my phone that I read the other sign attached to the wooden post.

DARTMOOR EROSION MONITORING PROJECT

The purpose of the post was not for taking selfies. It was for passersby to take photos to upload to the park authority's website for them to keep track of the erosion. And it seemed that the patch of land they were trying to monitor was the patch of land we had been standing on for the photo.

I decided not to upload that photo to their website.

We joined a section of the Two Moors Way – a long-distance trail linking Wembury on the south coast of Devon and Lynmouth on the north, via Dartmoor and Exmoor – and then shuffled carefully down the steepest hill of the day to a brook that forms the head of the River Avon. Rachel had her fifth fall of the day down this hill. This one in view of a couple out walking – the only people we had seen in over two hours.

We left the Two Moors Way just below the summit of Pupers Hill, before turning off and passing over its peak and along the top towards Ryder's Hill.

The terrain seemed to have eased as we climbed higher, and the ground felt drier. I was running along, innocently eating an apple when we reached a patch of muddy ground crossing the path. It was about a metre wide and the far edge looked to me like dried mud, so I instinctively tried to jump it. As my left foot made contact with what I thought was a solid surface, it disappeared through a top layer of crust and my entire leg vanished into the depths of the bog below.

The thick, muddy sludge had reached my knee, and my foot hadn't even touched the bottom. Fortunately, my momentum carried me forwards and my stomach landed flat on the grass on the other side.

All I could hear were Rachel's shrieks of laughter from behind me.

I had somehow managed to keep my apple clean, so lay there for a while laughing and allowed Rachel the opportunity for revenge to get a photo of me.

Just below Combestone Tor, we met a road for the first time in about four hours. It was a strange and quite unwelcome sensation to run on tarmac after the sponginess of the moor. We followed this road for a little over a mile until the village of Hexworthy, before turning off along a bridleway heading back west in the direction of Princetown.

We passed the remains of John Bishop's house. Not the Liverpudlian comedian, but a stonemason and labourer who built many of the stone walls across Dartmoor. He can't have been very good at his job because his house was in a pitiful state.

A giant radio and television transmitter sits on North Hessary Tor above Princetown. Its 196-metre-high mast is visible for many miles, and acts as a valuable waymarker (when there is good visibility). We were heading directly towards it but it didn't seem to be getting any closer. But for most of these final few miles we were on stony farm tracks and there was little risk of me disappearing into another bog.

We had covered 23 miles by the time we made it back to the hotel car park. This left us with the perfect distance remaining to run/walk 1.5 miles up the valley and back to one of Dartmoor's most popular attractions: Wistman's Wood.

Wistman's Wood is one of only three upland oak woods on Dartmoor. We visited as a family back in 2017 and it was one of the most magical places we had ever been.

The damp and mild conditions have created a temperate rainforest, which provides the perfect atmosphere for moss and lichen to cover all the trees and granite boulders. It dangles from the branches like tinsel.

We spent over an hour among the trees and even our three noisy children were silenced by the spell cast from the magic of the small but wonderful woodland.

When Rachel and I reached the woods as we approached the end of our marathon last Friday, we discovered the National Park had put up signs asking people to walk around the woods and not through them. The increased popularity of Wistman's Wood had damaged the delicate ecosystem and they had introduced the measures to prevent further damage to such a fascinating site. Perhaps a fenced route through the woods would have achieved the same goal but still given people the opportunity to experience its awe and wonder?

Viewing Wistman's Wood from the outside was not the same. We didn't get any of that feeling we had experienced the first time we visited and left a little disappointed. We had passed some foreign tourists on their way up to the woods. One of them was on crutches and I hoped their expectations were not set too high.

We were back at the hotel 6.5 hours after we started and went straight to the bar for a pint of Jail Ale before checking into our room.

It was the first time Layla, Leo and Kitty had been home alone for the night. We had left them with a Pot Noodle each (their dream meal), told them to feed the dog and cat and to be nice to each other. I'm not sure they even spoke to each other while we were away, as most of their communication seemed to be happening via our family group chat and consisted mostly of them arguing about trivial matters.

Rachel and I had a delicious meal and then Leo video-called us at about 10pm. He was just tucking in to his dinner – a few bowls of cereal.

'What about your Pot Noodle?' I asked. 'Did you have that earlier?'

'No. I had cereal earlier too. I decided not to have the Pot Noodle.'

He's 14.

'Do you mean you couldn't be bothered to boil the kettle?'

He didn't respond which gave us our answer.

I was wide awake from 3am the following morning. I was too hot, had restless legs and was very hungry. I debated cracking open a big bag of crisps we had brought with us, but I didn't think Rachel would appreciate it too much.

Soon after 5.30am, the sun was blazing through the curtains. It was a beautiful day and the idea of a pre-breakfast swim seemed very appealing. I did some googling and found a recommended spot a short walk from the hotel along the Cowsic River.

It was 6.30 when Rachel first began stirring, so I asked her if she fancied going to take a look.

'The cow sick river?' yawned Rachel. 'Cow sick? Really? It doesn't sound very appealing. I think I'll go back to sleep.'

'I hadn't even thought of Cowsic sounding like cow sick until you mentioned it.'

'It's literally what you're saying.'

'Well, I'm sure it's not literally a river of cow sick.'

'Fine!' she said. 'Let's go.'

We followed a winding path through stunning woodland, a short walk from the hotel. Rachel took off her shoes to walk along the cold, wet ground. Not because she wanted to be at one with the earth, but because her shoes had been rubbing during the marathon and left sore spots on her ankle.

We were uncertain which of the pools were suitable for swimming and they all looked a bit dark and shaded in the deep valley, so we retraced our steps back to the hotel instead. With ten minutes to go until they started serving breakfast, we had a quick dip in the icy moorland water of the West Dart, which flows directly under the two bridges of the Two Bridges Hotel.

I had set an alarm for 8.45am, worried that we might oversleep and miss breakfast.

By the time my alarm sounded, we were back at the hotel room, having already been on a 2-mile walk, had a swim in the river, eaten a full breakfast and packed our bags. It turns out a lie-in was a little optimistic.

Running a marathon across boggy moorland during a night away at a hotel probably doesn't sound like the most romantic way to spend 24 hours. But it made it all the more memorable, and the experience heightened our appreciation for the rest of our stay. That first pint tasted crisper, our meal felt more indulgent, our sleep seemed deeper and more restful (until 3am) and the morning swim and breakfast were all the more rewarding.

After an action-packed 24 hours, we were home by 10am on Saturday, ready for a quiet and relaxing weekend with the children.

'Who wants to come on a 10-mile walk with me?' said Layla.

'I need help with my maths homework,' said Kitty.

'Can you make me my Pot Noodle?' said Leo.

TOUR DE FRANCE - PART ONE

A 200-MILE CYCLING ADVENTURE

It might seem like Rachel and I regularly leave our children behind to go off on jaunts together. Admittedly, it was just two weeks ago that we left them for our Jog in a Bog night away on Dartmoor. However, before that, it had been over two years since we have been away without them. Plus, it's good for them to spend quality time with their grandparents, right?

For Rachel's birthday present this year, I booked us a three-day cycling trip to France. We would take the night ferry from Plymouth to Roscoff with our bikes on Thursday 16th May, spend two nights in France, and get the return ferry on Sunday afternoon.

This trip marked my third cycle trip to France. My first was with my friend Simon, when we rode from St Malo to Roscoff, and the second with Rachel to celebrate her 40th birthday (both feature in my book *Did Not Enter*). On each of these crossings, we were practically the only cyclists on the ferry. So, it was quite a surprise to arrive at the port in Plymouth at 9pm and find nearly 30 other cyclists, all heading to France with their bikes. Due to a technical issue with the loading door, there was a delay in passengers disembarking from the previous crossing. It was a calm, dry evening, which made the long wait more pleasant as we chatted with the other cyclists.

There was a group of four behind us. Two men and two women in their 60s. They were heading to Morlaix which is about 15 miles from Roscoff and were planning to spend a leisurely three days visiting the cafes, markets and restaurants.

'It's not very far, I know,' said one of them, slightly embarrassed. 'But it's an improvement from last time. Last time we only got as far as Carantec, which is less than 10 miles.'

'I think that sounds like a wonderful way to spend a few days,' I said.

There was another group of four men in front of us, all in their 50s, who cycled as a group regularly at weekends and had talked for years about going on a cycling weekend in France together but had never got around to it. And now they finally had, and this was their inaugural trip.

They all had panniers and were carrying camping equipment for three days, heading west along the coast towards Brest, and getting the same ferry home as Rachel and me on Sunday.

The eldest of the group, Jeremy, had heard there was a ceilidh in Brest on the Saturday night and was eager to incorporate that into their plans. The rest of the group were less keen and hoping they would be able to dissuade Jeremy.

One of the guys had somehow had a bike malfunction between the car park and passport control – a distance of about 50 metres. He had already found a bike repair shop near to the ferry port in Roscoff and was booked in for the Friday morning. Despite this less-than-ideal start to their trip, they were all in high spirits.

A young woman, probably in her early 20s and travelling alone, wheeled her bike up alongside us and nervously joined in the conversation we were having with the four men.

'You look like you're heading off on a long trip,' said one of the men. 'Where are you going?'

'Err... Milan,' she said coyly.

'Milan? As in Milan, Italy? Wow.'

'I know,' she giggled. 'It feels a bit weird.'

'How long do you think it will take you?'

'I've got a flight booked in six weeks.'

'So, are you cutting across France and then going over the Alps?' asked another one.

'Well... err... I've decided to head down the west coast of France first and then do a bit of the Pyrenees before going to the Alps.'

'The Pyrenees AND the Alps. That's incredible.'

'And then you're flying with your bike back to the UK?' asked Rachel.

'Er... no. I've got to fly to America for a family reunion and then I'm doing a road trip with my dad.'

Whereas the rest of us had driven our bikes to Plymouth from nearby towns, she had cycled about 50 miles that day from near St Austell in Cornwall. We all suddenly felt a bit pathetic.

'So has this trip been long in the planning?' I asked.

'No,' she laughed. 'I only decided to do it on Monday.'

'What? Monday this week?' It was now Thursday.

'Yes, I was in the pub with a friend, and I decided to head off on a trip this week so booked the ferry and my flight home. He was supposed to join me for the first few days, but he changed his mind.'

Not only was this her first time cycling abroad, but she also then admitted it would be her first time visiting France. Not wanting to rely on GPS navigation, she had a small scrap of paper with a list of towns to pass through on her journey south.

We were all in awe. We had been feeling excited about our various adventures. Three days cycling in France felt like quite a brave undertaking. And here we were chatting to someone who was heading off across Europe for six weeks on a trip she had only decided to do three days earlier.

Suddenly, we were the boring ones.

'That sounds incredible,' said one of the men, shaking his head. 'I'd love to do something like that.'

'Why don't you?' she asked.

'I can't,' he sighed. 'I've got to be at work on Monday.'

She then went on to tell us that from America, she hoped to get a place crewing a yacht from California to Australia. She had no sailing experience at all, but thought it sounded like a fun adventure.

It is amazing how quickly someone's life can change. We didn't find out much about her. We didn't even know her name. But she admitted she had been having a sort of midlife crisis, and a visit to the pub and a chat with a friend suddenly changed the entire direction of her life, and would potentially shape her future.

After a surprisingly enjoyable delay of over an hour, the cargo door was eventually fixed and they allowed the cars from the previous crossing to disembark, and we all shuffled forward onto the ferry.

I had a three-day cycle route all planned out for us. Well, I say that I had planned it. I googled *'three day cycle trips from Roscoff'*. The first result that came up said: 'Heading to Brittany? This 321km circular bike route from Roscoff takes in coastal towns and picturesque Breton villages.'

That would do.

I'd done a bit of cycling east and west of Roscoff but the inland route heading south was uncharted territory. 321km (199 miles) was quite ambitious for a two-and-a-half-day trip, but we decided to give it a go. If it turned out to be much more difficult than we planned, there was an option to cut the loop in half after the first day.

We had a cabin booked for our night crossing, but it wasn't ready when we boarded at 10.30pm, so we unfortunately had to go and have a beer in the bar while we waited. Unlike my trip with Simon when we foolishly had five pints before our long day's cycling, Rachel and I were very restrained and had just the one. And two family-sized bags of crisps.

The Brittany Ferries alarm music piped into all cabins an hour before the ferry arrives has become legendary in our house. It's a piece of Breton music by the band Dremmwell called *Troellenn*. It starts gently and is a calm and soothing way to be woken. But then the harp sounds quickly escalate into a lively and energetic jig. I was pretty obsessed with the track for a few years as it reminded me of holidays.

My family ridiculed me at the end of 2019 when the year's Spotify Wrapped (Spotify's personalised summary of each user's listening for the year) was released. Rachel, Layla, Leo and Kitty all had a cool and eclectic mix of songs and artists on theirs. My most listened to song on Spotify in 2019 was the Brittany Ferries alarm music.

So it was with great excitement that I drifted off to sleep on the Thursday night, as the boat gently rocked, knowing I would get the pleasure of *Troellenn* the next morning.

'WHAT'S THIS?' I shouted, as an unfamiliar bit of classical guitar music came through the speakers at 7am. 'THIS ISN'T MY SONG.'

'Really? Are you sure?' said Rachel, sitting up wearily in her bunk. 'It sounds the same.'

'Of course I'm sure! This is NOT the same.'

'I quite like this one. It's a bit more soothing than the other one. The other one was a bit... jarring.'

'JARRING? JARRING? ARE YOU SERIOUS?'

'Yes, sorry. It was just a bit whiney and irritating.'

'You're a bit whiney and irritating!'

'Grow up, George.'

The more I listened to the new one, the more I warmed to it. It had been a while since I heard the original and when I played it on my phone, I have to admit that it did sound a little, well, jarring, whiney and irritating.

I have had a couple more listens to the new one since - *Dihun – Le Réveil* by Carlos Núñez – and it too has become a favourite. I think we know what is going to be top of my Spotify Wrapped this year.

After coffee and pastries from the ferry's cafe, we untangled our trusty steeds from the mass of bikes that had been stacked together against the wall of the cargo deck. As about 30 of us climbed onto our bikes and edged towards the door ready to disembark, the last bike remaining was the woman who was cycling to Milan. She was so relaxed about her six-week trip that she was in no rush to get going.

We said goodbye to the different friends we had made in the ferry queue the night before and made our way through passport control. When we were the other side of the fence we looked back along the queue of cars and saw the Milan woman and her bike waiting in line.

'Good luck!' I shouted.

'Thank you. It was nice to meet you both,' she called back.

'I hope you make it to Milan,' said Rachel.

'And then America,' I added. 'And Australia!'

'Me too! Have a great trip.'

The weather forecast for our three days' cycling was somewhat uncertain, predicting intermittent heavy showers. But for now, the sun was out, and we were cycling through France. There's something uniquely exhilarating about cycling in a foreign land. It is a strange and wonderful feeling. Though it's essentially the same as at home, it feels entirely different and transforms a simple bike ride into an exciting adventure.

We followed the main road from the ferry port to Saint-Pol-de-Léon in the same direction as all the car passengers. But being France, there is a segregated bike lane the entire way.

Soon after passing through the town, we turned off onto smaller lanes and rode through sleepy little towns and villages, meandering through farmland with fields of onions and globe artichokes either side of us.

My previous cycling trips to France had been in early November and mid-March and rural Brittany had been noticeably deserted. I had assumed it was just quiet because of the season. But here we were, on a glorious spring morning, and there was still nobody around.

'Where is everyone?' I said as we cycled through the town of Plouénan at what should have been Friday morning rush hour.

'I don't know. Everywhere is so quiet,' said Rachel. 'This reminds me of that town we cycled to with the kids. The one with the supermarket. Remember it?'

'How could I forget? They only remind me of it at least once a week.'

We were camping in France a couple of years ago, at a lovely little site by a lake in the middle of nowhere. We had taken five bikes with us, and I suggested that it would be fun to go for a family ride together.

We were six miles from the town of Lapouyade that had, according to Google Maps, a supermarket. We could cycle there, have an ice cream and a drink, get some food for dinner, and then cycle home.

The temperature was in the high 30s and was fairly uncomfortable to cycle in. But the roads were deserted and the scenery beautiful and the reward of cold drinks and ice cream kept us all going.

When we arrived in Lapouyade, something didn't feel right. It was a beautiful place with immaculate streets and pristine houses. But it was completely empty and the whole town felt like it was CGI generated.

'Where is the supermarket?' sighed Kitty, who has never enjoyed bike rides.

'Just along this road, apparently,' I said, glancing at the map on my phone but starting to doubt it. Where Google Maps had a supermarket pinned, turned out to be a derelict barn.

'You said we were cycling to a supermarket!' said Kitty.

'I thought we were.'

'Surely there must be a shop here,' said Leo.

'Yeah, I'm sure there must be,' I said, totally unconvincingly.

We circled every street in that town. Let's be honest, it was a village, not a town, and after seeing the size of it, it's no wonder it didn't have a supermarket. I have checked and the supermarket on Google Maps is no longer listed. But I swear that it was.

Not only was there no supermarket in Lapouyade, but there was also no shop, cafe, nor restaurant.

Google Maps listed a farm shop about a mile out of town, so I left the rest of the family in the shade of the empty village square and cycled out to try to find it.

It did exist. But it was closed. I returned empty-handed to the rest of my disappointed family. We cycled back to the campsite in the blazing heat with Kitty sobbing and furious at me for 'lying' and 'tricking' her, and the rest of the family looking at me as though I had let them down big time.

Less than a mile from the campsite, when we were in touching distance of a swim in the lake and an ice cream from the campsite's small bar, when I thought we were over the worst of it, we encountered another problem.

We saw a warning sign with a picture of a wild pig and the words: *CHASSE EN COURS* - Hunting in progress

A couple of hundred metres further on, we passed dozens of men in full camouflage gear lined up along the roadside holding shotguns. There was a lot of shouting and rustling coming from inside the thick woodland, and the men with guns were all on high alert. Any moment a wild boar was going to burst through the tree line and be shot at by the hunters. This didn't do much to improve the morale of my family, and I've never seen them all cycle so quickly.

We made it back to the campsite alive and after a swim, ice cream and – because there was no supermarket for us to buy food from – takeaway pizza for dinner from the campsite's restaurant, I was just about forgiven later that evening. They still mention that bike ride regularly, as though I am in some way responsible for Google Maps' questionable data and France's wild boar hunting schedule.

To be continued...

THE KINGFISHER - PART FIVE

IF YOU ARE NEW to the adventures of the kingfisher, I wrote about its escapades in my book *Reconnecting*...

Here is a quick recap...

Rachel was given an ornamental kingfisher by her grandma for Christmas over 20 years ago. Since then, it has been passed back and forth between our family and Rachel's sister's family countless times in unexpected ways. It has been hidden inside cakes, easter eggs, a snow globe, a geocache and a Christmas bauble. It has made a surprise appearance at a honeymoon in Thailand and a wedding in California.

The kingfisher made its most recent appearance on Boxing Day last year, when Rachel's sister Miriam and her husband Eric discovered it tucked behind the fuel filler cap of their car, during a pit stop at Michaelwood Services on the M5 motorway.

We have been eagerly awaiting/dreading its return ever since.

Our family meet up with Miriam and her family about two or three times a year. The kingfisher often changes hands when we see each other, but not always. Sometimes the moment is not right and a visit will go by without it making an appearance.

Miriam, Eric and their three boys were coming to stay with us over the Easter weekend and it felt inevitable that the kingfisher would somehow be coming with them. After I had shared the story in my book, they probably felt a sense of duty to return it.

The tales of the kingfisher prompted many readers to get in touch with their own stories of similar traditions with friends and family. Would Miriam and Eric perhaps take inspiration from some of these? We were all on high alert.

They arrived on the evening of Good Friday, bearing a generous assortment of gifts, including wine, beer, prosecco, biscuits, chocolates, crisps, peanuts and packets of cereal.

'Oh my god!' squealed Kitty. 'REAL crisps and REAL cereal. Thank you! We only ever have the cheap Tesco own-brand stuff.'

'Poor you, Kitty,' I said sarcastically. 'You're so deprived.'

'We usually have the cheap own-brand stuff too, Kitty,' said Miriam. 'But this is a special treat.'

While the rest of the family eyed the goodies with delight, I looked at it all with suspicion. Every item in their bulging hamper seemed like a potential hiding place for the kingfisher.

An hour later, as Leo grabbed a box of his favourite Kellogg's Krave to begin his nightly ritual of cereal before bed, I watched on, half-expecting the kingfisher to tumble out of the packet into the bowl while he was pouring.

Later that evening, I cracked open both boxes of granola and had a good rummage through the contents. Both packets were clear.

On the Saturday, we enjoyed a coastal walk and a picnic lunch at the beach. Miriam had helped make the sandwiches and I suspiciously peeled back the bread of mine, wondering if an unwelcome visitor had been secreted inside, but all I found was cheese and coleslaw.

Rachel's parents treated us to dinner at a local pub that evening. When we arrived, there was no record of our reservation and the person who had taken the booking no longer worked there. Thankfully, while we all enjoyed a drink at the bar, they were able to make room for the 12 of us. As we were shown through to our table, I noticed Miriam having a whispered conversation with the barman.

I suddenly knew what she was up to.

Miriam must have sent the kingfisher ahead to the pub with the intention for it to be revealed to us somehow during the meal. But because of the mix-up with the booking, perhaps the instructions of the kingfisher had not been passed on either. Or maybe the kingfisher had disappeared with the former member of staff? Miriam was still having discussions with the barman.

Was it all over?

Was this the end of the kingfisher saga?

I then noticed that Miriam and the barman were now both smiling and nodding and seemed to have come to some agreement. It appeared that the plan – whatever it might be – was back on.

At every stage throughout the meal, I kept expecting the kingfisher to make an appearance. Rachel and I ordered a sharing platter between us, which was an assorted selection of tasty but mostly beige, deep-fried items of all shapes and sizes. Some of them were even ornamental kingfisher-sized. They couldn't have, could they? Biting into a piece of battered chicken, I did wonder if it would be possible to deep fry the kingfisher. Fortunately for me, and my teeth, it was chicken.

Dessert came and went, and the kingfisher had still not appeared.

I then found out that Miriam had actually been speaking to the barman about paying for a round of drinks, and the kingfisher had never even been a part of the conversation.

How had this stupid little ornamental bird made me so suspicious of everything?

Easter eggs were exchanged on Sunday morning. The kingfisher had already been concealed inside chocolate eggs twice in its lifetime, so it seemed unlikely that it would make a third. But maybe that predictability would make it somehow less predictable?

In a change to the usual Easter egg hunt, Rachel devised a fantastic multi-round challenge for the six cousins, inspired by the TV game show *Taskmaster*.

Each round required them to complete a different task and be judged by the taskmaster – me.

One of the challenges required the contestants to get a fresh egg as far away from a start line as possible, without crossing the line and without breaking the egg. Techniques included wrapping it in bubble wrap and hitting it with a tennis racket, attaching it to a skateboard and giving it a shove, and – the winning method – getting someone else to run off with the egg. Leo wrapped his in a couple of layers of tissue and then tried to launch it into a neighbouring field (having seen a video that suggested that eggs rarely break when they land on grass). Unfortunately for Leo, he focused too much on power, and not enough on accuracy, and mistimed his throw so badly that it powered straight into Eric's shoulder from about two metres away. Eric was a little shocked and bruised, but took it surprisingly well and his shoulder remained in one piece. The egg, however, did not. Leo received zero points for that round.

Another challenge asked contestants to put an egg in the most perilous position without it breaking. Entries included Kitty dropping it out of an upstairs window (it miraculously survived). Layla's was balanced precariously in a small box on a basketball hoop as a ball was thrown through it. One of the boys had his egg sitting in the driver's seat of the car with a can of beer and no seatbelt. Another had an egg sitting beneath the prongs of a tractor's spiky grabber (I'm not sure that's the technical term), surrounded by pitchforks and an axe. All were very creative, and I did wonder if there might have been an opportunity for the kingfisher to make a cameo. Yet again, it failed to appear.

For the final round, contestants were each given a hollow plastic egg that could be split into two parts. They had five minutes to put something inside the egg that would surprise me – the taskmaster – when opened. Entries included a slice of burger cheese, a Lego man, some sheep poo, a small bug crawling in a bed of garden greenery, and a pound coin, which was a blatant attempt at bribery – as if I would award points in exchange for money (I did).

This could have been the perfect opportunity to conceal the kingfisher. It would have been a snug fit, but I think it would have just about squeezed inside one of the eggs. But the game came to an end, awards were handed out and there was still no sighting of the kingfisher.

On the Monday, we went to the beach and braved heavy rain for 20 minutes and were rewarded for our persistence with blue sky for an hour. We played rounders, enjoyed a brisk dip in the sea and then indulged in another beach picnic. Again, I checked my sandwiches suspiciously. Again, they were kingfisher-free.

As the sky darkened and the rain clouds moved in again, we left the beach and returned home, had an early dinner and bid farewell to Miriam, Eric and the boys as they embarked on their long journey home to Northampton. The kingfisher remained elusive.

Following their departure, the hunt began.

They had to have left it somewhere. Surely, they would have used those three days as an opportunity to get the kingfisher back to us?

We searched the house from top to bottom. We stripped their beds, checked inside every drawer, behind every cushion, down the back of the sofas, and inside every cupboard. We scoured the garden and inside the van. We looked in bookcases, bathroom cabinets and plant pots.

'Maybe they didn't leave it,' I said, after 15 minutes of searching.

'They definitely did!' said Kitty. 'And I am going to find it.'

Kitty was relentless in her pursuit of the kingfisher.

'I reckon it's stashed in all this food,' she said, unzipping a cool bag in the kitchen.

We had tried to get them to take home some of the vast quantity of snacks they had brought down with them, but Miriam was adamant we should keep it all.

Was she too adamant?

She had even gone to the trouble of putting it all neatly into a cool bag and told us to take it with us on our Weekend in Cornwall with Storm Kathleen. Was she being kind and considerate? Or was she up to something?

'It's got to be in here,' said Kitty. '100% it's in this bag.'

Kitty pulled out the contents and began rummaging and inspecting all the boxes of biscuits and packets of chocolate bars. She then pulled open a multipack of McCoy's crisps.

'Kitty, I think you're taking it a bit too far now,' I said.

Undeterred, she began manhandling each individual bag in turn.

'Ah ha! Look! This one! It's much heavier than all the other packs.'

'Really?' I said, totally unconvinced.

She passed me the packet.

'Oh,' I said. 'You're right. That is way too heavy for a packet of crisps.'

'I knew it!' she said, tearing open the bag and revealing our familiar friend inside.

'Wow,' I said. 'That's impressive. How on earth did they seal it inside a bag of crisps? And how did you find it so quickly?'

'Because I'm a legend,' she said.

We sent a photo and a message on Rachel's family's group chat straight away.

'That was supposed to be for Cornwall!' replied Miriam.

The plan had been for us to take this bag full of snacks with us on holiday and discover the kingfisher while in our caravan or during a picnic on a Cornish beach. But our suspicion and Kitty's relentlessness meant that it only remained hidden for 20 minutes. We felt a bit guilty for ruining the surprise, but, to be honest, crisps never last very long in our house. It's inevitable I would have innocently opened those crisps later that evening. Especially as they weren't Tesco own-brand.

With the kingfisher back in our possession, we can't help but wonder what mischief it will get up to next. But one thing's for sure: it will be off on another adventure very soon.

Until next time...

Tour de France - Part Two

A 200-mile cycling adventure

The elevation map of the route Rachel and I were following had shown that the first 30 miles of day one would be mostly uphill. Having started at sea level, the road had been climbing very gradually, but having completed 25 miles, we had not yet encountered anything that could be described as a hill.

We skirted around the edge of Lac du Drennec, a man-made reservoir and popular spot for fishing and boating. We had camped on the other side of this lake for three nights a few years ago. There was an immaculately groomed sandy beach and beautiful clear water, so we stripped off and had a fantastic swim in our cycling shorts.

After drip-drying in the sun for a few minutes, we got dressed and cycled along the wooded shore of the lake for a mile or so before taking a right turn up through the trees.

I had downloaded a GPS file of the route to my watch, which meant a line on its screen showed me we were going in the correct direction and notified me if we strayed off course.

There are obvious positives about using GPS navigation: it's very accurate and efficient and means you get to relax and enjoy the scenery, rather than having to check the map regularly and spend the rest of the time wondering if you are going the right way. But a major disadvantage of using GPS is that you never really have any sense of where you are travelling through or near to, and only see your route through a very narrow window.

It would be entirely possible to be metres from something very exciting but know nothing about it because you've had no need to look at a map.

I tried to counteract this before we set off by taking a good look at the route we were following on a map. If I hadn't, we probably would have skirted around Lac du Drennec without realising it was where we camped a few years ago, and that it was a great spot for swimming.

I had also identified a really impressive church in one of the towns we were going to be cycling through – The Guimiliau Parish close – and I had made a mental note to stop and take a look when we passed.

'Where is that church you were going on about?' said Rachel.

'I wasn't going on about it. I mentioned it once. I think it must be coming up. Hold on, I'll check.'

I pulled out my phone and opened Google Maps.

'Oh,' I said. 'Apparently it was 10 miles back that way. We missed it.'

'Oh. How good did it look?'

'Definitely not 20-mile detour good.'

'Good.'

We had just been celebrating the lack of hills when the road began to climb significantly ahead of us. It was far less steep than the hills that surround our house in Devon, but whereas those are mostly short and sharp, this one continued for several miles.

Towards the summit, the name *GAUDU* was painted all over the road, in honour of popular French cyclist David Gaudu.

This hill formed part of the route of Stage 1 of the 2021 Tour de France. David Gaudu was the local's favourite as he was born and raised nearby.

Rachel and I were chatting together when a blue blur flew past us up the hill. It was a cyclist travelling faster uphill than we would have been if we were going downhill. He smiled and said something jolly in French, which probably translated as 'eat my dust, losers!' And then shouted 'Tour de France!'

'Tour de France!' I shouted back.

He continued powering up the hill and was soon out of sight.

'Maybe that WAS David Gaudu,' I said.

'Do you think it was?'

'Maybe. It did look a bit like him. If I had my name printed all over a road, I think I would probably choose to cycle that hill regularly.'

'Yeah, I suppose it would be good motivation.'

If you're going to be overtaken at speed up a hill, it feels better if they are an elite cyclist.

Five minutes later, another cyclist flew past us. This guy was about 70 and breathing heavily, but still travelling at twice the speed of us.

'Oh dear. Now I just feel really slow and unfit,' said Rachel.

'Maybe that was David Gaudu's dad.'

This stretch of road was the location of one of the most infamous moments in Tour de France history, when, in 2021, a young woman stood at the roadside holding a sign saying 'Allez Opi-Omi' (go, grandma/grandad). As the cyclists approached, she stood holding her message towards the TV cameras and her sign protruded into the road, clipped one of the bikes and caused a huge crash of over 50 cyclists, ending many of their races.

She then fled the scene, before turning herself into the police a couple of days later and being fined 1200 euros. There were calls for a tougher punishment to be issued and even talk of a prison sentence. I just felt incredibly sorry for her. Obviously, it was a careless thing to do, but there was no malice or intent. Imagine going to watch the Tour de France with a sign for your grandparents and then ending the race for many of the riders.

We were rewarded for the long climb with a fabulous long descent down the other side, with big wide roads, sweeping bends and no traffic to contend with.

Having learnt from previous trips through rural France, I knew it was a good idea to get food when you can as shops and boulangeries have a habit of closing for lunch, and then often not opening again for the rest of the day. Or week.

The lovely little town of Pleyben contained more people than we had seen during the rest of the day combined. It seemed that everybody from the surrounding villages was hanging out in Pleyben on Friday lunchtime.

We bought a curried chicken sandwich and a Tex-Mex chicken sandwich (when in France...) and ate them on a bench beneath the town's impressive cathedral. Probably not as impressive as the church we missed in Guimiliau, but it was an adequate substitute.

Still not quite satisfied, we returned to the bakery and bought a kouign-amann – a ridiculously big and dirty-looking pastry.

'I've just googled it and apparently kouign-amann is claimed to be the fattiest pastry in the world,' I said.

'You're the fattiest pastry in the world.'

'Grow up, Rachel.'

We ate half each and also shared a huge chunk of dense almond cake (you're a dense almond cake) that Rachel stated was one of the nicest things she'd ever tasted.

The road dropped down from Pleyben to meet the river Aulne, which forms part of the Nantes-Brest canal. Built in the early 19th century, this canal stretched for nearly 240 miles across inland Brittany via 238 locks. It fell into disuse during the 1900s and only a few sections remain navigable by boat. But the towpath has become a popular route for walkers and cyclists, bringing a much-needed tourism boost to towns and villages close to the canal.

About a mile into the ride, we reached a 'route barrée' sign – road closed. Our day was already going to be over 85 miles and any sort of detour to avoid this closure could add significant mileage. But if we ignored the sign and then found that it was impassable a few miles further on, this would add even more miles with us having to backtrack.

We decided to risk it and hoped that we would either be able to pass by the closure or act the ignorant tourists. Which wouldn't be too much of a stretch.

Another mile further up the track, we spotted a couple of construction vehicles in the distance, and it looked like some resurfacing work was going on. As we approached, we remembered that this was France which meant nobody was actually there. The vehicles and machinery sat empty, and we carried on our way. We noticed this a lot all over rural France. Tractors, lorries, diggers parked up mid-job, with no sign of any work being done. I imagined these construction workers and farmers all sitting in a nearby cafe somewhere (probably Pleyben), enjoying an extended lunch break on a Friday. And who could blame them?

The gravel path followed the course of the river around many long sweeping bends, past locks and old lock-keeper's cottages. We followed this track for about 15 miles to Chateaulin, a pleasant town straddling both sides of the river.

'Do you fancy an ice cream?' I asked Rachel.

'I would quite like a coffee,' she said. 'What about you?'

'A coffee sounds good.'

We propped our bikes against the wall of Maison Le Roy, and I went inside to order two coffees. When I came back outside, Rachel was about to sit down at an outdoor table. There were two other women sitting under the shelter of the canopy.

'Non, non, non!' one of them said, shaking her head and pointing up to the clouds and then gesticulating for us to go back inside the cafe.

We looked up at the sky. It did look a little threatening but didn't seem too imminent. Rachel smiled, said 'merci' and took a seat. The woman then got even more animated and, assuming we didn't understand, began theatrically miming rain and wind with her arms. It was quite the performance.

'Maybe we should drink them inside,' I said to Rachel.

'OK, fine.'

I smiled and nodded at the lady, 'Merci, madame!'

We took a seat at a table inside and before I had even had a first sip of my coffee there was an almighty clap of thunder and an impressive flash of lightning.

The two women from under the canopy had now also moved inside and the one who had warned us raised her eyebrows and smiled, with the international sign for 'I told you so.' We thanked her again.

It began raining heavily and the thunder and lightning intensified. Cycling along the canal, we hadn't passed any form of shelter in 15 miles, so the timing of our cafe visit had been extremely fortuitous.

Half an hour later, the rain showed no signs of stopping, so we ordered a second coffee and waited it out.

An hour after we set foot in the cafe, the rain finally eased, and we climbed back on our soggy bikes and continued onward.

The toughest hill of the day greeted us within half a mile of leaving Chateaulin, as the road climbed steeply out of the river valley.

On this higher ground, we passed hailstones piled up at the roadside. If we had not stopped in Chateaulin for a coffee, we would have been caught in the hailstorm on this exposed hilltop with thunder and lightning. We both felt very lucky. Little did we know, but our luck would run out tomorrow.

The town of Locronan describes itself on its welcome sign as 'le petite cité de caractère' – the small town with character. The route we were following skirted around the town, but with such a bold claim, we decided we should ignore our GPS and take a detour to check it out.

And we are very glad we did.

Locronan was the prettiest village we passed through on our entire trip. With its cobbled streets and beautiful granite houses, it felt like we were walking through a meticulously crafted film set. During the 15th to 18th centuries, Locronan became a centre for the production of hemp, which was used to make sailcloth and ropes for the navy. Locronan's sailcloth was highly valued and contributed significantly to the town's prosperity. It is now a very popular tourist destination.

We pushed our bikes through the cobbled streets and then cycled out of town, before realising we had taken the wrong road and had to walk the cobbled streets for a second time. It turns out I wasn't very good at navigating when not following our GPS.

It might seem like I am always out doing long bike rides, but in reality, I do very few. My previous French cycling trips with Simon and Rachel were back in 2018 and 2019. Other than one long ride with Simon last August, I had not cycled more than 35 miles in nearly two years. And Rachel had done even less than me. Three back-to-back days totalling 200 miles was going to be a big challenge for both of us.

To be continued...

MAKING DREAMS COME TRUE IN YELLOW AND BLUE

THE STORY OF ABINGTON STANLEY FOOTBALL CLUB

AFTER SPENDING EIGHT MONTHS driving around the United States (see *Not Tonight, Josephine*), Rachel and I returned to our hometown of Northampton. We settled into a series of dull jobs, but life was pretty good. We moved into a 'cosy' flat together and had a big group of friends whom we saw most weekends.

One Saturday afternoon, while in the pub with four of my friends – Damo, Mark, Jim, and Tom – talking about football (we rarely talked about anything else), an idea was born.

It was the summer of 2003. We had been participating in five-a-side football every Wednesday evening for years but liked the idea of playing more competitively. We considered joining an already established Sunday League team but realised it was unlikely all five of us would get to play regularly together. None of us was blessed with any footballing ability, so there was a strong likelihood we would end up warming the substitutes' bench each week. This thought didn't appeal too much.

There was another solution.

We could start our own football club. And, if we were in charge, we would get to decide who the players were, and we could make sure the five of us were picked every single week.

We contacted the General Secretary of the local Sunday league and were invited along to a meeting. Damo, Tom and I attended, expecting a casual chat where we gave them our contact details and paid the relevant league fees. Instead, we faced a formal interview with the league's secretary and chair.

'So, do you have your committee established?' she asked, pen at the ready.

'Yes, absolutely!' I lied. 'It's all sorted.'

'And who is the club's chairman?'

'Er...' I looked at Tom and Damo, who both unsubtly pointed back at me. '...Oh, yeah, that's me. George Mahood. I am the chairman.'

'Ok, that's great. And who is the club secretary?'

I looked around again, and Damo and Tom were pointing back at me. I shook my head this time and gave her Damo's name instead. Damo rolled his eyes and mouthed the word 'dick' at me.

'And the treasurer?'

'That'll be Tom.'

Tom let out a big sigh.

'And have you appointed a manager?' she asked.

'Yes! That will be me,' said Damian proudly. 'I am in charge.'

'Well, technically the chairman is in charge,' she said.

I wiggled my eyebrows at Damo, gave him a smug grin and mouthed the words 'you are my bitch!'

He mouthed the word 'dick' again.

It had been Damian's lifelong ambition to be a football manager. When I first suggested the possibility of setting up a football club, he shouted out 'bagsie being manager' before I had even finished the sentence. His credentials? He had once taken Charlton Athletic to the European Cup Final... in *Football Manager* on the Commodore 64.

After the meeting, Jim, who had been unable to attend the meeting because of... well, something very important presumably, gave himself the honorary title of Director of Football, which meant absolutely nothing. Mark decided he didn't want an official role. He just wanted to play football.

'Well, I might not even pick you for the team,' said Damo.

Mark just laughed. And he had a point. We weren't exactly inundated with players.

Just as we were leaving the meeting, the league's secretary spoke again.

'And you need at least 12 players registered before the start of the season. Is that ok?'

The three of us looked at each other, startled.

'Twelve? Do you need the names now?' I said, unsure that I even knew 12 people who could kick a football, let alone 12 who would want to join our team.

'No, just as long as you have them all registered by the deadline. Which is next Saturday.'

'Oh.... Ok.'

'You do have 12 players who will sign, don't you? Because we can't accept the football club into the league if you don't have enough players.'

'Oh yes, we have plenty of players. SOOO many players. Don't you worry.'

In truth, we only had five players. The same five who had been in the pub when the idea was formed. We had a little over a week to recruit another seven.

Over the next few days, we contacted all our friends and then friends of friends and somehow managed to scrape together 12 players just before the deadline. Two of them lived in different counties, over an hour's drive away, but said they were happy for us to sign them up. Such was the lure of our special new football club that these two travelled to matches every single week for many years.

We called our football club Abington Stanley. It was named after the area of Abington in Northampton where we all lived, and Accrington Stanley – one of the oldest English football league clubs, made famous by this TV advertisement for milk in the 1980s. To us players, the team was always known as The Stanley.

We knew we weren't going to be the best team in the league, but we were hopeful we wouldn't be the worst. Having checked the league standings from the previous season we noticed a team called British Rail FC who had lost all of their matches, with a goal difference of -160. Surely, we would be better than them? Unfortunately, we never got to find out as British Rail FC folded just before the start of the 2003/4 season. British Rail (the government-owned rail provider) became defunct in 1997, so it's a miracle that their football team kept going another six years.

We acquired old goal nets and corner flags from a disbanded club and inherited an old kit from my brother-in-law's former team. It was blue and black stripes, like the Inter Milan kit, and had *PIONEER* blazoned on the front. Not the big electronics brand, but a slightly dodgy pub in Northampton.

Midway through our first season, we purchased an impressive new kit – yellow shirt, yellow socks and blue shorts. Jim came up with our club's tongue-in-cheek motto – *Abington Stanley: Making Dreams Come True in Yellow and Blue.*

With our fancy new club colours and a healthy financial investment from a wealthy backer (a National Lottery grant), we went all out with the club merch: training tops, hats, drinking bottles, keyrings and mugs. I still use my mug most days.

It took Abington Stanley a while to get going. It was ten games before we had our first win. And that was a cup match against a team from another town that were unable to field 11 players.

We were at the bottom of Division Eight of the Northampton Sunday Combination. There was no Division Nine, so we had nowhere to be relegated to. Which was oddly comforting.

The average age of our team was considerably older than the teams we played against, who were made up predominately of young and sprightly 18- and 19-year-olds. We could usually match them for fitness for about 30 minutes and then we would dramatically fade away and inevitably concede several goals in quick succession.

We rarely had any substitutes. Some weeks, we didn't even have 11 players, so we often had to rope in various friends or relatives at the last minute. All players had to be officially registered with the league, and when a team fields an ineligible player, it's known as a ringer. If caught, the team faces points deductions, fines, and potential disqualification from the league. Ringers are usually skilled players from another team brought in to gain an advantage. This was never the case with Abington Stanley. None of our ringers was registered with any other teams, and most had never kicked a football in their lives. We gained no advantage whatsoever, other than having 11 bodies on the pitch.

We would brief our new, illegal player before the game, giving them the name and date of birth of one of our actual registered players, just in case they received a booking and the referee asked for details for their match report. We need not have bothered. Our ringers rarely touched the ball, let alone did anything that would warrant intervention from the referee.

Abington Stanley were serial winners, however. We won a trophy three years in succession. The Fair Play Award, which was awarded to the team who received the fewest yellow and red cards during the season. This meant we were effectively the nicest (some would say 'most pathetic') team in the league.

There were plenty of other highlights, as this extract from *Life's a Beach* shows.

Mahood on fire as Stanley shatter Real

DIVISION EIGHT
GEORGE MAHOOD got his 2006 off to a flying start as he hit a hat-trick to inspire Abington Stanley to a 9-0 hammering of struggling Real Roochers Reserves.
Rob Wright and Ben Laylock both hit doubles, while the scoring was completed by Alex Lacey and Al Soto.
Double Top also rattled in...

The proudest moment of my football career – probably my life – came when our local newspaper ran a full-page article on the week's local football results, under the headline MAHOOD ON FIRE AS STANLEY SHATTER REAL. My team – Abington Stanley FC – had recorded our biggest ever victory against a struggling bunch of no-hopers, and I had scored a hat-trick.

I had reached my footballing wonderland. If you ignore the reality that this was a local paper desperate for stories and forget that we were second from bottom of Division EIGHT of the Northampton Sunday Combination league (there was no Division 9) and overlook the truth that the 'Real' it refers to is not Real Madrid but Real Roochers Reserves who regularly conceded 10 goals or more, then it was a pretty special moment.

The rest of the team used to joke that the photographer for the local paper – *The Chronicle and Echo* – had a bit of a thing for me. Because whenever Abington Stanley featured in their roundup of the weekend's local sporting action, it was usually accompanied by a picture of me. Not because I was ever doing anything special on the pitch (that hat-trick happened once in 10 years), but more likely because I played in the centre of midfield so was usually involved in the play and also close to the photographer who was stationed on the halfway line. I also had big, stupid hair, which made me an easy target.

SLIDING IN – Abington Stanley take on Piddington Saxons in the Combination last weekend

ON THE CHARGE – Abington Stanley against Gunners SA

Stuart Cooper reports on the action

GETTING STUCK IN – The Cock v Abington Stanley

We had a food sponsorship deal with the local pub, which some of us would retire to after the match. They would provide us with big platters of chips and deep-fried leftovers from the night before, and we would sit and watch the Sunday lunchtime football on the TV. After a couple of beers, I would wander home across the park and Sunday afternoons passed by in a blur, with regular naps on the sofa. This was in the years before having children. After our children were born, Rachel would often walk down to our local pitch if we had a home game – The Stan Siro, or Le Stade de Stanley as we affectionately called it (officially, pitch 14 of Northampton Racecourse) – to watch the game and let the children play in the park, and then we would walk home together after the match.

I wasn't a very good footballer, but my commitment to the team was never questioned. I missed all six weeks of my banns readings before our wedding because it clashed with Abington Stanley's fixtures. The first week I was due to go to church and I got a text from Damo saying we were short of players (we were always short of players), so Rachel told me to play. The same thing happened the next week (would you believe it?) and then the next, and then Rachel told me not to bother going to the remaining church sessions.

Another time, I persuaded Rachel to let us cut short our holiday in Devon and drive home ridiculously early on a Sunday morning to get back in time for a 10.30 kick off. She reluctantly agreed. We lost the match 9-0, and I did question whether it had been worth it.

As Chair and Secretary, Damo and I shared most of the roles between us. Phoning around trying to find referees each week, booking and paying for pitches (they had no email or phone, so it had to be done in person) and attending the regular tedious league meetings. We would arrive at the pitch just before 10am on a Sunday to put up the nets, and the rest of the team would arrive over the next half-hour in various states of sobriety and sleep deprivation. Back then, 10am felt ludicrously early. Having children quickly changed my perception of what constituted early morning. I now play football at 8.30am on a Sunday, and that is after a lie-in.

We played on various council-owned pitches around Northampton, of varying conditions. There were usually a selection of dog poos to avoid and discarded fireworks to clear up before kick-off. We turned up to a pitch one Sunday morning to find the centre circle occupied by the burnt-out remains of a car. The referee, seemingly unbothered by the obstacle, told us to just play around it. Another time, a referee, who was clearly nursing a hangover, wanted to call the game off due to a 'waterlogged' pitch. In reality, there was just a big puddle in one of the goalmouths, and he wanted to go home. Our players, determined to play, got down on our knees and used branches and our hands to brush as much water away as possible. Begrudgingly, the referee allowed the match to go ahead.

After one particularly bad autumn storm, we arrived at the pitch to find half of it ankle-deep in leaves. As long as we could see the lines, the referee was happy for the match to proceed. So, our team warm-up consisted of raking leaves from the pitch with our hands and feet.

One of my least memorable moments (quite literally) came during a pre-season friendly with AFC Grasshoppers. I went up for a header on the halfway line after a goal kick. At the same time, one of their players also jumped for the ball. Neither of us made contact with the ball, but both made heavy contact with each other's heads.

And then all the lights went out.

The next thing I knew there was a strange man in a green paramedic uniform leaning over me. I was lying on the grass with other players standing around me.

'What's the score?' I said, trying to sit up. 'How long is left?'

'Don't move just yet,' said the paramedic, 'stay where you are. You've been unconscious for a while.'

It turns out that clashing heads with the other player had knocked me unconscious. I then fell, lifeless to the floor and hit my head again on the hard ground, which resulted in me having a seizure for several minutes. It was pretty traumatic for the rest of my teammates who watched on as my eyes rolled back in my head and I convulsed on the floor. An ambulance was called and a nearby first responder arrived within minutes.

The match was abandoned (much to the annoyance of the opposition who were 1-0 up at the time), because we started the match with 11 players and with Damo coming to hospital with me, we were down to nine.

I was kept in hospital overnight for monitoring and discharged the next morning. I was playing again a couple of weeks later but tried to avoid headers (especially headers into other player's heads) for the next year, just to be on the safe side.

Abington Stanley continued for four more seasons after I moved to Devon. I had dreams of making occasional guest appearances whenever I was back in Northampton, and maybe sharing the pitch with Leo in an Abington Stanley shirt one day. But the team sadly folded when the secretary and manager stepped down and nobody wanted to take their places.

Looking back, I feel proud to have been part of the original five who decided to set up Abington Stanley Football Club. It's one of my proudest achievements – helping to build a club that played for 14 glorious but glory-less years. Despite our lack of trophies, victories, or basic football skills, it was a journey filled with laughter, lifelong friendships, and many happy memories. We created something special with that club. A club that brought a group of no-hopers together and made dreams come true in yellow and blue.

TOUR DE FRANCE - PART THREE

A 200-MILE CYCLING ADVENTURE

An indication of how much I am struggling and how tired I am during a bike ride or run is the number of photos I take. We had another 15 miles of cycling after leaving Locronan before getting to Quimper, our destination for the night. According to our map, we passed through the villages of Plogonnec and Guengat but I don't remember anything about either, and didn't take a single photo during those 15 miles.

It's the same when I'm running a marathon. I take lots of photos, but it's very rare for me to take any during the final few miles, when my head is down and I'm just going through the motions until it's all over.

Having only seen a handful of cars on the roads all day, it was strange to be waiting at several sets of traffic lights in the big city of Quimper. Our hotel was a couple of miles the other side on the outskirts, and we knew we wouldn't want to walk or cycle back into the centre later that evening, so climbed off our bikes to do some sightseeing. This involved a short wander through the pedestrian streets and an incredible ice cream by the river. Quimper – tick.

Our accommodation for the night was a budget one-star hotel ironically called Première Classe. But it was cheap, had a bed and a hot shower, which was more than enough.

The hotel was next to a branch of Buffalo Grill, an American-themed steakhouse chain, popular across France. We first spotted them back in 2015 when we travelled to Vichy for me to take part in my ironman (did I mention I've done an ironman? I don't like to talk about it much). We saw branches of Buffalo Grill dotted all along the autoroutes as we drove through France and thought we should give it a try sometime. The night after the ironman, on our way back to the ferry port, we stayed in a hotel next to a Buffalo Grill and had steak, chips and beer which was one of the best meals of my life. Not because of the food, but because of everything that had happened in the previous four months leading up to that ironman. Buffalo Grill became a firm favourite with our three children, particularly as they serve candy floss for dessert, and we have visited several times over the years. None of our subsequent visits came anywhere close to that night after the ironman.

Layla, Leo and Kitty were angry enough with us as it was, travelling to France without them, so it felt like a betrayal to go to Buffalo Grill. Instead, we walked on by and ate a kebab in a kebab house next to a drunk man swigging vodka from a bottle in between shouting angrily at the staff.

It was 8.15pm when we left the kebab house and we called into a supermarket to buy some beers to take back to the hotel. The alcohol aisles had been roped off for some reason (perhaps because of the guy in the kebab house?), so we settled for crisps and chocolate and returned to the hotel for an early night.

Day two didn't get off to the best of starts. I had foolishly washed my cycling shorts and cycling jersey in the shower the previous day, before checking to see whether the radiator in the room worked. It didn't. I optimistically hung them up to dry, but they were still soaking wet in the morning.

I then sleepily walked to the hotel lobby and bought two coffees from a vending machine, spilled one inside the machine, so had to buy a third. I was then told off by the man at reception for not wearing any shoes.

We were on the road again by 8.20am. The man who told me off appeared in the car park, smiling this time, pointed at our bikes, gave a thumbs up and then said, 'Tour de France!'

'Oui,' I said, giving him a thumbs up in return. 'Tour de France!'

We passed the kebab place we had eaten at the night before and are fairly sure the same vodka-swigging man was sat at a table outside. What a night he'd had. Taking a side street directly opposite the kebab place, we were back in the countryside in less than a minute.

The road undulated through beautiful woodland, passing the town of Saint-Evarec, before reaching the coast at La Foret-Fouesnant and then into Concarneau from the west. We had successfully cycled from the north coast of Brittany to the south coast. A distance of about 100 miles. All we had was the small matter of another 100 miles north before our ferry home the next day.

We had visited Concarneau on a family holiday before, but all I remembered was the historic walled old town and a busy port. I was not expecting to find a stunning white sandy beach, which was imaginatively called Plage des Sables Blancs – white sand beach.

My soggy cycling shorts had just about dried in the early morning sun, but the sea was so calm and inviting that we couldn't resist having a swim. There were a few others already in the water and we spent ten minutes floating around enjoying the slightly warmer temperature of the Bay of Biscay compared to the English Channel.

We got changed and I hung Rachel's soggy pink sports bra to my backpack and assured her it would be dry in no time.

Concarneau's old walled town sits on an island in the harbour, accessed via a bridge. This historic area, once a fortification and stronghold during numerous battles and sieges since the 15th century, is now predominantly filled with shops and restaurants, making it a popular spot for tourists. We decided to forgo the old town's breakfast options – like foie gras tartelettes – and ventured out of the centre in search of something more affordable and casual.

Both of us were feeling hungry and grumpy (mostly me) as we slogged up a long, steep hill out of town, regretting our decision to bypass all the touristy food outlets in the old town and bustling port area.

Our perseverance was rewarded at the top of the hill with a large boulangerie called Avellann – with the confusing slogan: fille de la lande et du vent – which translates as 'the daughter of the moor and the wind'. I'm not sure what that's got to do with a bakery, but it was clearly working as the place was very popular.

We bought a couple of slices of quiche, two large doughnuts (one apple and one toffee) and two cups of Seattle's Best Coffee (when in France...) and sat on the grass verge in the car park to eat. It's perhaps not a normal sight outside a French bakery, as one man laughed and said something involving the word 'picnic'. Another lady smiled and then said something which we didn't understand and then she laughed and said 'Tour de France'.

'Oui,' I said. 'Tour de France!'

The French sure are obsessed with the Tour de France.

From Concarneau we cycled on to the pretty town of Pont-Aven. It's been a popular destination for artists, including being a favourite of Paul Gauguin, and it is understandable why. The river Aven winds its way through the boulder-strewn landscape, past mill wheels, willow trees and footbridges, before emptying into the quaint harbour. It's a stunning spot. Rachel's main interest in the town was that it had a public toilet.

A long, slow climb out of Pont-Aven took us back out into the open countryside. The deserted villages on Friday made me think that perhaps everyone was just busy at work, and that we would notice a big difference on Saturday. I was wrong. Other than the tourist traps of Concarneau and Pont-Aven, there was nobody else around.

We bought a couple of filled baguettes from a boulangerie in Bannalec with the intention of saving them for later, but they looked so good that I ate most of mine in the time it took Rachel to put hers in her backpack.

'I thought we were saving those for later?' said Rachel.

'I cwouldn't wesist,' I said.

Rhododendrons are taking over this part of France. The beautiful, but highly invasive, plant is spilling out of woodland, hedges and roadside verges in glorious shades of pink and purple. It made for very pleasant cycling, but this part of Brittany will soon just be one giant rhododendron.

We passed through the quaint little villages of Saint-Jacques and Kergaouen (didn't see a single person in either of them) before joining a cycle path at Scaër that would follow the trackbed of an old railway for 23 miles, all the way to our destination for the night – Carhaix-Plougher.

Like in Britain, the decline in rail use and the increased popularity of the car saw thousands of miles of railway lines across France disbanded in the 1960s. But unlike in Britain, France seemed to keep most of the land in public ownership and built a vast network of 'voies vertes' – greenways – along former railways and tow paths. In Britain, the short-sighted government instead chose to sell vast tracts of the former railway land back to private landowners, making the process of turning them into greenways much more difficult.

After about 30 minutes, we stopped at a bench next to the trail to eat our lunch. The rest of mine was gone before Rachel had taken her first bite. Sitting there, in the shade of the trees, and the birds deep in chatter all around us, we were marvelling about what a fantastic day's cycling we were having. There were some dark clouds looming ominously in the distance, but we had no idea how quickly our fortunes would change.

To be continued...

The Dog Next Door

The Story of Tan the Sheepdog

About eight years ago, Tan, a border collie puppy, arrived at the farm where we live. She was brought in to be trained as the farm's new working dog and would live in a kennel in the farmyard in front of our house, along with Rose, an old and semi-retired sheepdog.

Tan was nervous and skittish for the first few weeks, unsure of her new surroundings, but she soon settled in.

Our dog, Ludo, arrived on New Year's Eve 2018. By this point, Tan was about two years old and obsessed with the new kid on the block. She spent her time sitting on our garden wall, watching Ludo with fascination. The two have been best friends ever since and Tan joins us on almost all of our daily dog walks around the neighbouring fields.

The sheepdog training didn't go quite to plan.

Although Tan clearly possessed a natural instinct to stalk and herd sheep, she was never very good at it. She and Rose were more interested in trying to herd our cat Moomin, and the many others that live on the farm.

Last year, the farmers where we live sold all their livestock and started leasing the fields to neighbouring farmers instead. This meant that Tan became unemployed.

This is not a sad story about a dog no longer having a purpose.

This was when Tan began her glorious retirement.

As well as the usual local walks around the countryside, we started taking Tan further afield. In her eight years, she had rarely left the farm.

I have never seen such a happy dog as that first day she visited the beach. She spent several hours in a heightened state of alert, checking out all the new dogs, people, sights, and smells. We couldn't get her to leave.

From that moment onward, Tan sort of decided that she was part of our family. She enjoyed her days out so much that often when we opened the door of the van to take the kids to school in the morning, she would jump straight in and sit on the seat as if to say, 'I'm ready! Where are we off to today?'

The room where I write has a stable door and I leave the top section open most of the year to let in light and fresh air. If it's been a few hours since I've taken Tan for a walk, she will often stand on the other side of this door and bark until I take her out again.

In the summer, when we leave the kitchen door open, she will wander into my study and sit next to my desk and stare at me (or bark) until I take her out.

One morning a few months ago, Rachel and I woke up early to be greeted by this face peeking around our bedroom door upstairs.

Layla and I were out on a long walk with Ludo and Tan a couple of months ago. We met a group of horse-riders coming towards us, so stood in to the roadside with the dogs to let them pass.

'Morning,' said a young cheerful woman on the second horse.

'Morning,' we replied.

'Is that Fucking Tan?' she asked. 'It is! It's Fucking Tan!'

Layla and I looked at each other and laughed.

'Er... yeah, it is,' I said.

'Hi, Fucking Tan! Good to see you, Fucking Tan. How are you doing, Fucking Tan?'

Layla and I stood at the roadside looking startled. We were four miles from home and had no idea Tan had gained this reputation, let alone been known to anyone outside the farm.

'Bye, Fucking Tan!' she said, as she trotted on up the road. 'See you soon, Fucking Tan.'

We later found out that Fucking Tan had acquired her nickname during lambing season, when she was supposed to be assisting with moving the ewes from one enclosure to another. Instead of doing what she was instructed to do, she herded the sheep wherever the fuck she liked, making the whole process far more difficult than it would have been without her. The farmers vocalised their frustration: 'That fucking dog! Fucking Tan!' The woman we saw had kept her horses in a stable next to where the lambing took place, so had often witnessed the antics of Fucking Tan.

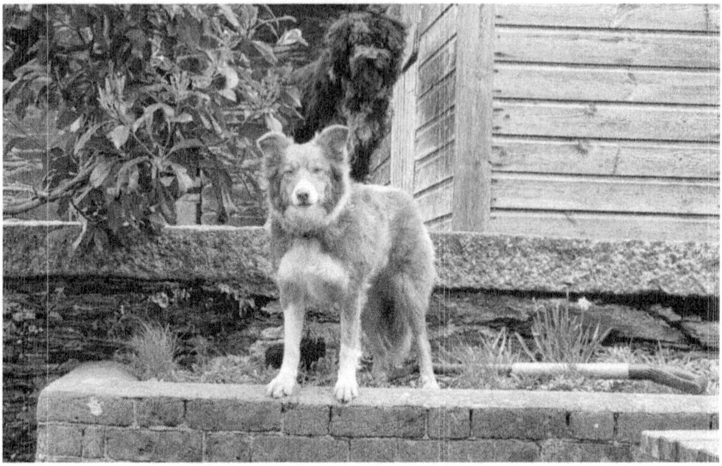

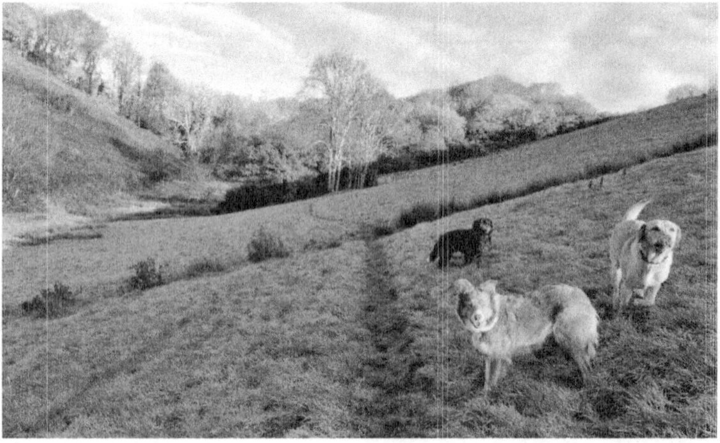

MAKE FUNNY

Tan gets regular exercise and lots of excitement from all our excursions together, and we enjoy spending time with her, without all the responsibilities of owning another dog. Everyone is very happy with the arrangement. Except Layla, who constantly tries to convince us to adopt Tan. Here is Layla's birthday present to Rachel earlier this year.

Tan and I have a special bond. Every time she sees me lacing up my walking boots outside our house, she races straight over, barks excitedly and sticks her nose and obscenely long tongue in my face. She seems very fond of me and I am very fond of her.

There's a certain trust and understanding between us, built over hundreds of miles of walks together. Tan knows when I'm about to take her out even before I've finished getting ready. Her eyes light up, and her entire body language changes, showing just how much she enjoys our time together.

Our relationship changed dramatically a couple of weeks ago.

I was out walking my usual loop with the dogs, and I passed through a gateway about a mile from home. Next to the gate was a rook scarer – a device designed to frighten off birds from the crops. It had not been there the day before. The dogs were curious of this new, mysterious contraption on our walk, but knowing what it was, I encouraged them past it as quickly as possible.

When we were about 10 metres beyond it, the rook scarer went off with a sudden, deafening bang. Ludo rushed over to me and stood closely to my legs. Tan did the same, and I gave them both some affection and tried to reassure them it was nothing to worry about. Milo, our neighbour's big and boisterous Labrador who also joins us for walks, wasn't in the least bit fazed by it and bounded up to the rook scarer wanting to check it out. I called Milo away, and as we headed off across the field it went off again. Milo bounded up to it excitedly like before, Ludo squashed even closer to me, but Tan this time raced off across the field in the direction of home.

We finished the walk and Tan had made it home safely and was sitting in her kennel. She seemed okay and was happy to see me.

The following morning, I took all three dogs out for a walk again, this time to a different field, far away from the rook scarer. Five minutes into the walk, Tan turned and fled. I didn't hear a noise, and neither Milo nor Ludo reacted, but it's possible Tan had heard it again from across the fields. Later that day, I took the dogs out again. This time, Tan only made it as far as the end of the driveway before turning and heading back.

The next day, she was out in the yard and excited to see me, but when Ludo, Milo and I began walking up the driveway, she refused to come with us.

The next morning, Tan wouldn't even leave her kennel when she saw me.

I decided she just needed time.

A couple of days later, I met our neighbour in the yard. She had just got back from walking the loop with Tan and Milo. The crop had been harvested, the rook scarer was no longer there, and Tan had walked the whole way without any bother.

I called Tan over. Usually, this was her cue to bound over to me, looking for some love and affection. Instead, she looked up, made brief eye contact with me, and then skulked off to her kennel.

She has obviously associated the trauma of the rook scarer with me and holds me fully responsible. It feels like I have let her down big time.

This was two weeks ago.

She's now happy for me to go and pet her but still won't come for a walk with me. If she sees me in the yard, her head drops and she creeps back to the security of her kennel.

It's going to take a long while to win back her trust, but I'm determined to do it. I'll have to try to build it back gradually, and hope I'll get to see that needy, loving face of hers sitting next to my desk again soon.

Tour de France - Part Four

A 200-mile cycling adventure

With just 20 miles to go until we reached Carhaix, our destination for the night, we were enjoying a leisurely cycle along the old railway line. It was still only mid-afternoon and we talked about stopping for a beer in the next town we reached.

Many old stations, train sheds and signal boxes line the route. Some have been turned into cafes, museums and homes, and others lie abandoned. We had stopped to look at one of them when a violent pattering like machine-gun fire intensified over to our left. Seconds later we were being pelted by large hailstones.

We cycled quickly towards the trees for cover and failed to find any that provided much protection from the relentless onslaught. It's the first time I have ever been grateful for my helmet for protection from hail.

At this point, we should have taken the time to put some extra layers on, but my raincoat was strapped to the outside of my rucksack and now already soaking wet, and Rachel's was buried deep in the bottom of hers. It still felt quite mild so we assumed we would dry off once the hail passed.

The hail then turned to heavy rain for ten minutes as we crouched beneath a pathetic-looking tree, soaking us further. And then it stopped as quickly as it began.

'I'm feeling quite cold now,' said Rachel.

'Me too,' I said. 'I think we'll warm up once we get going.'

After the failed attempt at washing my clothes and then the swim in the sea, my shorts and shirt were now soaking wet for the third time today.

Not only was Rachel's pink sports bra wetter than it had been when I tied it to my bag in Concarneau, it was now splattered with mud too. As were both of our backs and bums, making it look like we each had a giant skidmark.

The rain stopped, the sun came out and it felt like we were over the worst of it. Shortly before reaching the town of Gourin, a flash of lightning lit up the sky, followed by a crack of thunder so loud it made me swerve my bike. I usually love thunderstorms, but this one was far more intense than anything I'd ever experienced. Then the hail began again, even more vicious than before.

We came to a stop and took shelter at the side of the path. Another flash of lightning and another roar of thunder followed.

I laid my bike down on the verge and stepped away from it, realising that holding onto a large metal object during an electrical storm was probably not a good idea. I suggested Rachel do the same. At that moment, another crack of thunder erupted, and Rachel flung her bike violently to the ground, where it landed heavily on its rear derailleur.

'WHAT ARE YOU DOING?' I shouted.

'WHAT DO YOU MEAN, WHAT AM I DOING?' she retorted.

'You're going to break your bike!'

'I'm trying to stay alive! I think that's more important than my bike!'

'It's not one or the other! You could have put your bike down gently. You didn't need to throw it!'

'Well, SORRY for caring about my own safety over my bike. My bike wouldn't have been much use if I was DEAD! Are you saying my bike is more important?'

'Of course not. Stop being so dramatic. It would just be annoying if your bike got broken for nothing.'

'So it would be OK if my bike got broken as long as I got struck by lightning too?'

'Now you're just being silly.'

Fortunately, Rachel's bike had landed on soft grass and was undamaged. And of course I'm relieved that Rachel didn't get struck by lightning either.

Having discarded our bikes, we then argued about where was the best place to stand during an electrical storm. Neither of us fancied lying on the wet floor (apparently this is not a good idea anyway – crouching is better), and there was no sign of shelter nearby. Standing under a tree is rule number one of things not to do, but the trees were all relatively small and seemed low risk, so we stayed where we were.

'I'm just glad I don't have a nose piercing,' I said to Rachel.

'You really can be a dick sometimes,' she said.

It eventually eased and the lightning passed. Minutes after getting back on our bikes, we passed a very surreal scene – a flock of camels in a field (yes, that is the correct collective noun. Or 'caravan' can be used, but that tends to be for travelling camels). They were the most miserable camels I've ever seen, which is not surprising considering the weather. I can't imagine they have to deal with too many hailstorms in France or their native country.

We were both shivering violently when we reached Gourin. It was a town big enough to have a cafe or shop for us to warm up in. But we were far too wet and far too muddy for any establishment to have welcomed a visit from us. Plus, we were only 12 miles from our destination for the night, and it felt like if we stopped somewhere now, and the weather didn't improve significantly, then we might never leave again. With a commitment to be in Roscoff by 2.15pm the following day, we couldn't afford to cut short our day's cycling, so reluctantly passed through Gourin and hoped we would warm up soon.

The following two hours were two of the most miserable either of us had experienced on a bike. It gave us a whole new appreciation and longing for basic home comforts. The previous day, as we pulled into Quimper for the night, we had debated whether to have a beer or an ice cream first. But now, beer and ice cream were the furthest things from our minds. All we wanted was a shower, a dry change of clothes and to be warm again. Fortunately, our 'evening wear' was wrapped securely in a plastic bag inside our backpacks, and the anticipation of knowing we wouldn't be cold and miserable forever kept us going. I could almost feel the comfort of a clean, dry T-shirt and a pair of boxer shorts. Then my heart sank as I remembered we only had one pair of shoes each, and water was squelching out of mine with every pedal stroke.

'Oh no!' I said.

'What?' Rachel asked.

'Our shoes! Even when we're dry, we'll have to put these trainers back on when we go to get food.'

'Oh gross. And tomorrow morning,' she added.

Even our bikes were moaning. They were grinding heavily, with the chains, cogs and brakes all clogged up with dirt and gravel.

I tried to look for some positives. The heavy rain had washed some of the mud from my shoes, and my backside was not as muddy as it had been half an hour earlier. That was about all I could think of. And I kept reminding myself that we were still on a cycling holiday in France. We had little cause for complaint.

We eventually rolled into Carhaix just before 6pm after 68 miles, absolutely shattered, dripping wet, and caked in mud.

I had been emailed the access code for the hotel side door and given instructions of where to store our bikes, so I was hoping to sneak up to our room undetected. Unfortunately, the lady at reception caught sight of us and dashed outside to intercept us.

There was no jolly 'Tour de France!' exclamation this time. She looked at us and let out a big sigh.

Carhaix-Plougher is a popular town for cyclists and is the intersection of five different bike routes, so we can't have been the first to turn up looking like we did, but it wasn't the most welcoming reception we've ever received.

She led us round to the back of the hotel to the bike garage and the pleasing sight of a hosepipe. We washed most of the mud off the bikes and cleaned our feet and legs. Rachel's bum and back were coated in mud, but she insisted it did not need spraying. When she turned to leave, I sprayed her anyway, and then did my own.

Up in our room, we showered fully clothed and then rinsed off our shoes and kit as best we could in the bath.

We thought of the four guys we had chatted to in the ferry queue who were carrying all of their camping equipment. The idea of being as cold, wet, muddy and miserable as we were and then having to pitch a tent and potentially have nowhere to shower or rinse our clothes, made us feel very grateful to have the luxury of a hotel room.

We also thought of the young woman cycling to Milan and wondered how she was getting on with her own journey. Part of me was still envious of her six-week adventure, the other part of me was glad our trip was only for a few days, and I was looking forward to the comforts of home.

Feeling clean and dry (apart from our shoes), we headed out to find somewhere to eat, and settled on a quiet little bistro called Le Tire Bouchon (the corkscrew) where we had a charcuterie board and a chicken burger each. Rachel declared it was one of the nicest things she'd ever eaten, but she had cycled 68 miles and then downed a large beer followed by half a bottle of red wine, so I would take her culinary review with a pinch of salt. Personally, I preferred the kebab in Quimper.

Rachel couldn't even hold the camera steady

Foolishly declining dessert, we left the restaurant and Rachel went back to the hotel while I walked for 20 minutes around Carhaix trying and failing to buy chocolate. It was 9pm on Saturday evening and everywhere was closed.

After a decent buffet breakfast at the hotel the following morning, we retrieved our bikes from the garage and cycled through the empty streets of Carhaix. We rejoined out friend – the converted railway line of the V7 – which we would be following for nearly 40 miles to Morlaix.

The surface of the greenway was mostly crushed stone, with occasional muddy or rocky sections. It was beautiful to cycle along and spared us from dealing with steep hills, but it didn't feel particularly French. Being surrounded by nature and away from road traffic was wonderful, but it's an experience you can also find in the UK. Each time the path passed a farm, a house, or an old signal box converted into a gîte, it gave us those little glimpses of French life which were the real highlights of the trip.

At one point, the route emerged from the trees into a small hamlet. Across a field to our left, we saw a quaint church and what appeared to be a stall in the car park, possibly selling food or drinks. Seeing lots of people milling around, we assumed it was a market and turned off onto a gravel track leading to the church. As we got closer, it quickly became clear that it was a private gathering, not a public market. A giant St. Bernard barked aggressively at me, and I quickly turned my bike around. Rachel, with better eyesight and better judgement, had already turned around and was waiting back on the road. The dog chased after me, its barks growing angrier and more threatening as it snapped at my ankles. One of the men made a half-hearted attempt to call it back, or maybe he was encouraging it to chase me. Thankfully, St. Bernards are not known for their speed, and I soon put some distance between the dog and me and rejoined Rachel on the road.

'Yeah, I decided maybe we shouldn't go down that way,' said Rachel.

'Thanks. Nice of you to tell me,' I replied.

We were soon back among the trees following the course of Le Squiriou river north.

I am never fully relaxed when cycling abroad. Especially with the deadline of a ferry to catch. In the back of my mind, I am always worried about some sort of mechanical failure and being too far from any civilisation to get the bike fixed in time. After my previous cycling trip with Simon along sections of the Eurovelo 4, I knew that some parts might not be suitable for road bikes. I even considered bringing along a folded spare tyre in case it was needed. However, Rachel dismissed the idea, saying, 'Decathlons are everywhere in France,' based on her extensive experience of seeing the huge sports stores from the passenger-seat window during countless miles of driving on French autoroutes. So, I left the spare tyre and chain repair tool behind.

We had cycled nearly 200 miles in France without encountering a single Decathlon.

As our bikes rattled over rocky terrain, bouncing over tree roots and navigating ruts, surrounded by dense forest stretching for miles, I silently prayed to the cycling gods, hoping our bikes would hold together until we got to Roscoff.

'Oh god, it feels like my bike is about to fall apart,' Rachel exclaimed.

'Don't worry,' I said, 'Decathlons are everywhere in France.'

'Alright, you can stop saying that now. I admit, Decathlons are not everywhere in France.'

The path grew busier as we approached Morlaix, bustling with runners, walkers, and fellow cyclists enjoying their Sunday morning. We encountered numerous cycle-tourers, heavily laden with panniers, embarking on their own adventures, many likely having arrived in Roscoff that morning on the ferry. It's quite amusing to think of British tourists greeting each other in French, strongly suspecting the other is also a tourist, yet not confident enough to say 'morning' instead of 'bonjour'.

The forecast rain held off and we reached the town of Morlaix – 15 miles from Roscoff – in good time. Two slabs of salted caramel pastry from a patisserie gave us a much-needed energy boost for the final stretch along the stunning coast road, past Carantec and on to Saint-Pol-de-Léon.

We had been given strict instructions from the children to bring back Milka chocolate and Babybel cheese from our trip to France. Both of which can be bought at our local Tesco, but both of which apparently taste better from France.

It was 12.38pm when we pulled up outside the supermarket. It had closed at 12.30pm.

'The kids are not going to be happy with us,' said Rachel.

'I'm more concerned about what we are going to do for lunch.'

We cycled the remaining miles down into Roscoff, past the ferry terminal and into the town centre. A car boot sale was underway in a grassy park by the waterfront, so we strolled our bikes around to take a look. For some reason, I expected a French car boot sale to be classier and more sophisticated than a British one, but it was reassuringly just as crap.

One of the bakeries was open, so we bought two filled baguettes each.

As we ate the first of our baguettes in the ferry queue, I felt a sense of immense satisfaction wash over me. We had conquered over 200 miles of beautiful French countryside in two and a half days. It had been another memorable cycling trip, and already, the more challenging moments had faded, and been overshadowed by everything else we had experienced.

The four guys we had chatted to on the outbound ferry rolled into Roscoff shortly after us, all with big grins spread across their faces, and full of stories of their own adventures. There is a simple but unique joy in getting on a bike and exploring new places. And doing so in a different country takes this feeling to another level. I was already getting excited for future trips.

Fortunately, they sold Milka chocolate in the onboard shop, which helped appease Layla, Leo and Kitty, when we returned home later that night. And it turns out they can't tell the difference between French Babybel cheese and the same bought from Tesco.

TALES FROM A CONFERENCE CENTRE

WRITING BOOKS CAN BE a lonely existence. While I have interactions with readers and authors via email and social media, actual real-life face-to-face human contact with others in the industry is very rare.

There are, however, occasional opportunities for real-world connections. Last week, I made my annual pilgrimage to London for *The Self Publishing Show Live*.

I attended the inaugural event in March 2020, two weeks before the first Covid lockdown. Several hundred of us squashed into a conference centre for two days and then onto a barge on the Thames for the evening party. I loved it. I turned up not knowing anyone, feeling completely isolated in my work life, and left with a renewed sense of optimism (and a slightly heightened sense of impending doom, and perhaps a tickly cough).

The event didn't happen in 2021 but returned in June 2022 and then again in 2023 and 2024. I have been to them all and am now the proud owner of four lanyards.

I was in two minds about whether to go this year. The cost of the ticket, train travel, and two nights' accommodation is quite high, in addition to taking up three days of my time. Three days I could spend writing, or, more likely, procrastinating and searching for food in the kitchen.

However, I remembered the buzz I experienced at the previous three shows and the draw of chatting with fellow authors and immersing myself in the publishing world for a few days. It was too strong to resist.

The conference was scheduled to start at 8.15am on Tuesday with an informal meetup at a pub the evening before, so I got an early train from Devon to the Old Smoke on Monday last week.

Whenever I visit London on my own, I make a pact with myself to avoid public transport and walk everywhere instead. Partly to save money, but mostly because London is so much better above ground.

For those of you who are new to my books or this newsletter, my wife Rachel and I have, for no discernible reason, run a marathon every month since January 2020. With just over a week left in the month and no marathon completed yet, I decided to embark on an impromptu London Marathon, combining sightseeing and ticking off June's goal in one go.

It began with a five-mile walk from Paddington Station to my hotel on the South Bank, via Hyde Park, Buckingham Palace, St James's Park, the Palace of Westminster, the London Eye... and McDonald's. My London geography is appalling, so I am always surprised to stumble upon famous landmarks as I haphazardly try to navigate across the city.

I dumped my bag at my hotel, changed into my running shorts, and set off east along the Thames, with no real idea of where I was going. I would just follow the big river. How hard could it be?

Well, for a big river, it was surprisingly easy to lose, as the Thames path kept wandering away from the water through back streets, parks and residential areas.

Running along the Thames sounded wonderful in theory. But I had underestimated just how busy the South Bank gets when the sun is out. Walking was a challenge, let alone running.

Further east, the crowds dispersed as I passed Tower Bridge, through Southwark and Rotherhithe and then on to Greenwich.

I remembered passing the Cutty Sark on my first ever marathon – the real London Marathon – in 2009. I didn't know much (anything) about it but always assumed the Cutty Sark was some iconic sailing ship used in battles. Perhaps during the Napoleonic Wars or even the First World War. It turns out it is famous for transporting tea very quickly from China to Britain. It was built in 1869 and was, at the time, one of the fastest ships in the world. I love the thought of engineers teaming up to build a faster boat just so tea could get to us quicker. What I love even more is that for the 150 years since, we have celebrated this ship, displaying it proudly to the world, because it brought us our tea quicker than ever before.

London is often grey and overcast when I visit. I hadn't anticipated the hottest day of the year so far, and the running conditions were fairly uncomfortable. I walked a lot and stopped regularly to enjoy the sights as much as possible. It could not have been more different to my April marathon which took place in Tesco car park, or May's which took place in a bog on Dartmoor.

I visit London twice a year at most. Each time I do, a small part of me wishes I lived there. But the bigger part is glad that I don't. It is an incredible city and its energy and charm are captivating. But after a few days, I am always ready to return to rural Devon.

Savouring a few minutes of cool air as I crossed under the Thames via the Greenwich Foot Tunnel to the Isle of Dogs, I then headed west along the North Bank, skirting past Canary Wharf, through Limehouse and Wapping. The crowds grew thick again as I reached the Tower of London.

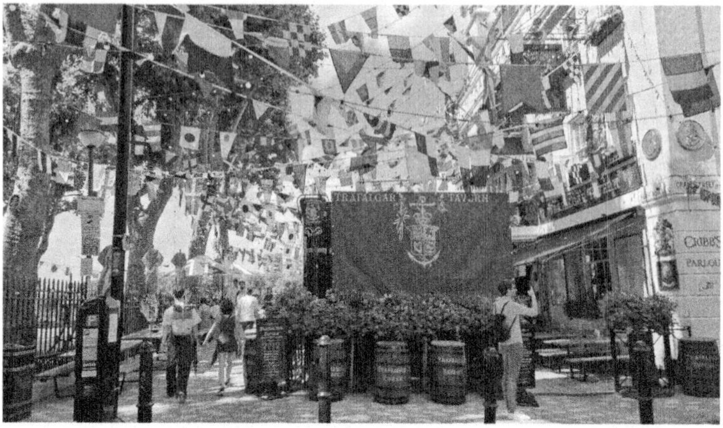
CRIBB'S

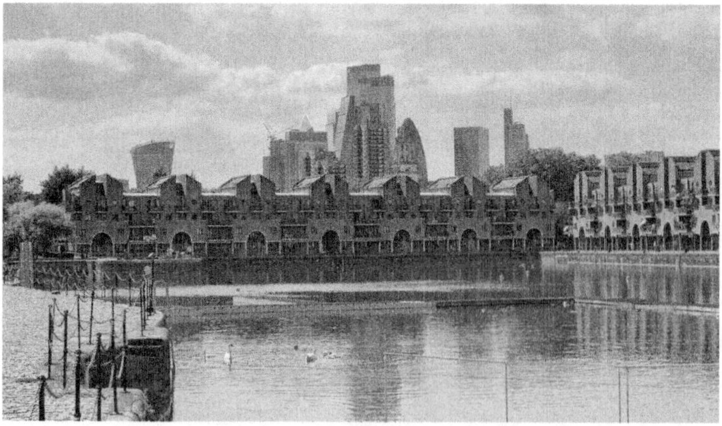

The section along Victoria Embankment brought back memories of my first ever London Marathon. Wondering why the hell I had signed up to do something so stupid, urging that finish line to get closer, and longing for it all to be over. About 75 marathons later (I don't know exactly how many I've done), I still feel the same towards the end of each one and this was just as hard as that very first.

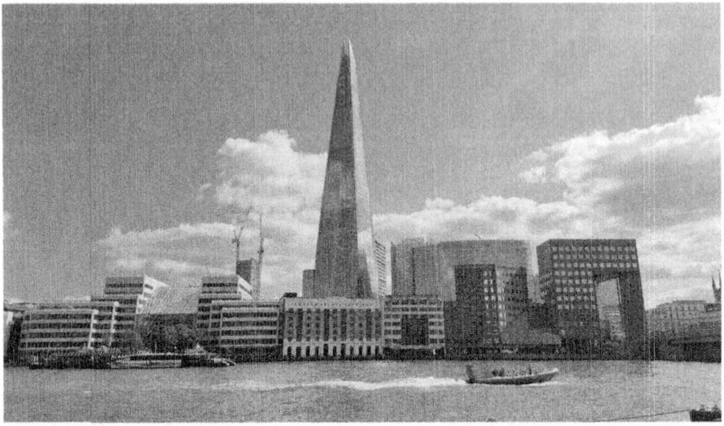

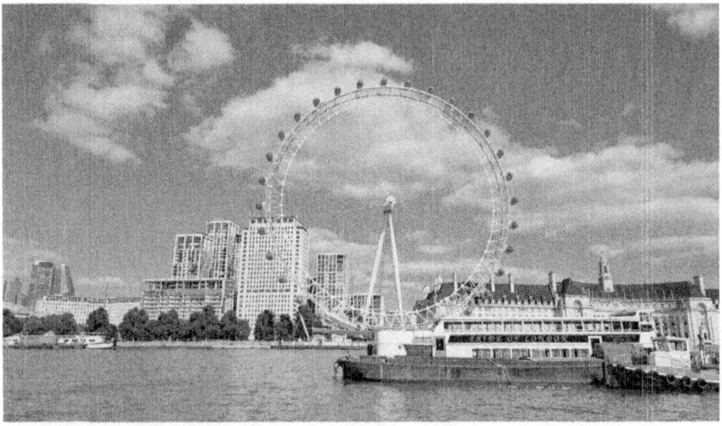

I picked my way through the crowds and preachers on Westminster Bridge and returned to the South Bank with just three miles left to run. At the 25-mile point, I was really struggling, so bought a kebab which I ate while walking the final mile back to my hotel. Still hungry, I then bought a meal deal which I took up to my room, before realising I didn't have a fork or a spoon. To make matters worse, I then remembered I had done the very same thing last year.

Sitting there in my hotel room in my pants, eating a falafel salad and yoghurt with a tourist bus flyer as a makeshift spoon, I did wonder if I perhaps wasn't cut out for city life. Or life in general.

I had a very quick shower and change of clothes and headed out to the pre-show get-together at a nearby pub.

It was reassuring to spot a couple of familiar faces and I spent the next four hours chatting to different authors, reminding myself why I had come to London. My legs were done for the day, however, and I had to use the bar as support for the entire evening.

After a restless night, tossing and turning because of the heat and my angry legs, I was at the South Bank Centre at 8.15 the following morning.

The conference is attended by a fantastic mix of seasoned professionals and newbies. There were many established authors at the top of their game, and there were many others just starting out, yet to publish their first book and new to the industry. I probably sat somewhere in the middle. Over a decade into my self-publishing 'journey' and fortunate enough to be able to call myself a full-time author, but still with a lot to learn.

The talks covered a wide range of topics. There were several sessions about audiobooks. Artificial Intelligence and its impact on the industry played a prominent role. There were presentations about selling books directly to readers. There were inspirational panel sessions from monumentally successful authors like EL James (*Fifty Shades of Grey*) and Lucy Score (*Things We Never Got Over*) who have sold a staggering 180+ million copies between them.

During the breaks and lunch hour I chatted to all sorts of random people. I met dystopian thriller authors. I met cyber punk, post-apocalyptic, cosy mystery and steamy romance authors (and some combining all these genres in the same books). I met LitRPG authors, self-help authors, Gothic, sorcery and gaslamp fantasy authors. And one who makes a killing from a book called *Things To Do While You Poo On The Loo*. Each conversation was a reminder of the vibrant and varied world of self-publishing.

Day one's schedule of talks came to an end. After a short break, the large bar area of the conference centre was given a makeover. The lights changed colour, a band set up, the free drinks were poured, and it became the venue for the evening after party.

It had been a pretty exhausting day following a late night, little sleep and early start, and then a full schedule of talks and chatting. It was a shock going from not speaking to anybody about books and publishing for a year, to suddenly speaking to everyone about everything. The marathon the previous day might have had an impact too. I wasn't sure I could handle another four hours socialising, so, at 8pm, I made my apologies to the American sci-fi author I was chatting to and wandered off to try to find out if the rumours were true that they had set up a TV for those wanting to watch England vs Slovenia in the Euros.

The rumours *were* true.

There were three others sat in a booth at the far end of the conference centre, hidden around a corner, watching a TV with the sound turned off and the commentary displayed in delayed subtitles. I sat down and planned to have a break for five minutes before making an effort to be sociable again.

Three hours later, I was still there.

Not because the match was so engrossing (it was truly awful, but surprisingly more enjoyable with the sound off), but because I was very happy to dial things down for a while.

And also, because the other people I was sat next to were so nice and interesting.

I spent most of the time chatting to a man who was at the conference in the role of 'husband'. He had worked all his life as a civil servant and then his wife Yvonne had written a series of murder mystery books that had really taken off. Now he was working full-time for her (or coming along to conferences, drinking free beer and watching football). At about 10pm, she too got tired of chatting and came to join us in the antisocial zone.

Yvonne was still reeling with embarrassment from an earlier incident. She had been walking around Covent Garden the previous day looking for a 'Pause the Menopause' march that was taking place.

She had heard that some of the marchers were going to be dressed up as female body parts and was filming a Facebook Live video as she walked.

'I am looking for a giant vagina,' she said proudly to her Facebook fans on her hugely popular page, Growing Old Disgracefully.

During the conference, at a particularly quiet and inappropriate moment, she had accidentally knocked her phone on her lap, and in the deathly silence of the auditorium her phone blared out the previous day's video.

'I AM LOOKING FOR A GIANT VAGINA!'

Her husband (Mr V, as he likes to be mysteriously known) said his initial instinct was that some Just Stop Oil protesters had stormed the building, before realising the commotion was from his own mortified wife sitting next to him, who was frantically fumbling with her phone trying to make it stop.

I also chatted to a woman named Sharika who is just about to publish a series of illustrated children's books based on her own real-life adventures (Maya's Worldly Wonders).

There were another two guys, friends from university, one a successful traditionally published author of young adult books, the other with a background in business. Together they had decided to set up their own publishing company. I still feel like I am figuring things out, but when they found out I had published my first book 12 years ago, they wanted me to tell them everything I knew about self-publishing. I was suddenly an expert. An industry veteran.

It was 11.30pm when security eventually made us leave our little booth as the venue was closing. I said goodbye to my new friends and headed back to my hotel.

After a more successful night's sleep, it all began again early the next morning.

I am so glad I made the effort to attend. It was well worth the money and time invested. I didn't necessarily learn a great deal of new things this year. But I see that as a positive. It means I am doing a lot of things right.

The overriding message emphasised the importance of being human, connecting with readers, and adapting to change. There's still a lot I need to work on – mostly the mundane business admin stuff – but even that excites me.

Strangely, there was no mention of Substack in any of the talks. This could mean I'm heading down the wrong path completely. Or – and I prefer this interpretation – it means I am way ahead of the curve, and by this time next year, all the talks will be about how Substack is the place to be. Am I right? [taps microphone] *Is this thing on?*

The real value for me came from the personal connections and shared experiences with others. When I talk to Rachel about anything to do with publishing, she does her best to feign interest, but I can tell her eyes are glazing over (this is despite her being a published author). If you've read this far, there is a good chance your eyes are glazing over too.

To suddenly be surrounded by hundreds of others who all understand, who all get it, is an incredible feeling. Over a week later, I am still on a high.

Last year, I filled a little notepad with lists of things to act on and implement. Just before heading to London this year, I stumbled upon that same notepad, untouched since then.

This year I took notes again.

But this time it is different.

I've already taken action on some of those points. And some of the ones from last year. Over the past 18 months, there have been many moments when I struggled to believe that this career path could continue to be sustainable. I feel very differently now. This is where I want to be. This is what I want to do for many years to come. And I'm going to knuckle down and make it happen.

It was suggested that this year's *Self Publishing Show Live* would be the last. However, in the closing talk, it was announced that it would return again in some form in 2025. I will be one of the first to buy a ticket. But I definitely won't run a marathon the day before (I probably will).

Until then, I'll be here, writing, publishing, and connecting with all of you.

Two Months Alcohol-Free

Two months ago, while lounging on the sofa watching TV, I wandered over to the fridge to grab a beer. It was 9pm on a Monday.

For the last few years, I've tried to moderate my alcohol and avoid regular weekday drinking. But this was a Monday during the school holidays, so those rules didn't really apply.

I knew that beer would probably lead to a couple more, and then Tuesday would still be part of the school holidays, giving me a free pass to go again. My rules were very flexible, and I seemed to be creating more and more exceptions to my self-imposed moderation policy. Holidays didn't count. Social engagements didn't count. If we had something to celebrate, if there was half a bottle of wine left open from Sunday, or if it was a particularly nice sunny day, those didn't count either.

My Relationship with Alcohol

I've always had a fairly amicable relationship with alcohol. I drink regularly, but not to excess, and I'm quite a fun drunk (at least, I think I am).

But in the last few years, I've felt that this relationship was changing.

When Rachel and I go out, either to friends' houses or to a pub that's not within walking distance, I am almost always the designated driver. I won't have anything to drink, and I'm absolutely fine with that. But then we'll get home, and I'll often have a beer to compensate for not drinking while we were out.

And while I am usually restrained enough to avoid drinking midweek, I find myself looking forward to Friday so that I can crack open that bottle of wine.

I have also noticed how much alcohol is disrupting my sleep. Alcohol works as a sedative and tricks you into thinking you have had a good night's sleep, but it's not the same restorative sleep you get without alcohol.

I don't suffer too badly from hangovers, but often in the days following heavy drinking, I notice a general lethargy and a fog that clouds my mind. I was also attributing my lack of energy, motivation and productivity to my drinking. It certainly wasn't helping.

The Decision to Take a Break

There was no grand reason or logic for deciding to take a break from alcohol. I had considered it a few times in the past, but there was always a reason not to. *Christmas is coming up. We are going on holiday next month. It's my birthday soon. My friend's having that barbecue. Maybe I'll stop after that wedding.*

But there was never going to be a right time. So, I put the beer I was holding back in the fridge and haven't had any alcohol in the last two months. It wasn't necessarily going to be for good. I was just taking a break. Conducting my own experiment to see what all the fuss was about.

The Final Drink

I almost feel that I should have ended in style. Gone out on a three-day bender, waking up in a pool of vomit, swearing I would never drink again. It would have felt more justified if my last experience of alcohol had been a bad one.

Instead, my last night's drinking – which, at the time, I didn't realise was my last night – was pleasant and quite typical. A nice, cold beer while cooking dinner and then half a bottle of red wine in front of the TV. It tasted great, and I woke up the next morning with no obvious side effects.

The Expectation vs. Reality

I thought this would be the post where I told you all that I'm a changed man. That giving up alcohol was the best decision I ever made. That I now sleep like a baby every single night and wake up each morning raring to go. I imagined myself telling you how my productivity and motivation have improved dramatically and that I am emotionally more balanced than ever and how everyone keeps telling me that I am a joy to be around.

But the truth is, I have yet to see any of these benefits.

Not a single one.

My sleep is still disrupted. I wake up most mornings feeling like I've had a few drinks the night before, even though I haven't. There has been no improvement to my energy levels or motivation.

And I'm as emotionally unstable as ever.

As for productivity? I don't think it's made any difference whatsoever. In fact, I think this post would have been much better and more interesting if I had written it when I was drinking (although if I had it would have all been a lie).

Sobriety Fatigue

Surprisingly, I haven't missed alcohol as much as I thought I would, and it has therefore been easier than I expected.

The first two weeks were quite tough. Not because of the cravings or the desire to drink, but because I was strangely feeling more tired than ever. This phenomenon is known as sobriety fatigue – even for non-regular drinkers, it apparently takes the body three or four weeks to get used to not having alcohol regularly in the system.

Two months on, this overwhelming fatigue has gone, but I certainly don't feel any more energised than before I stopped drinking. Surely by this stage, I should be noticing some benefits?

Saturday Night Smugness

It is very rare for me to go to bed sober on a Saturday night. I am used to waking early on a Sunday morning, either to take Leo to his football or for me to play football. The first Saturday after taking a break from drinking, I went to bed feeling unbelievably smug.

'I am going to be fucking awesome at football tomorrow morning,' I thought to myself. 'The other guys are not going to believe what a legend I am.'

Did it work?

Not at all. Not only did I feel just as rough when I woke up, but I played worse than ever.

Assuming it must have just been a blip, I went to bed the next Saturday feeling equally smug and optimistic. The same happened the following morning and I've had a series of dreadful performances one after the other.

It's entirely possible that the alcohol-induced fog I used to play football with gave me an illusion of playing well, and that maybe I've been this terrible all along. Now I am just seeing what everyone else has always seen.

Social Stigma?

I went on our annual football night out a few weeks ago. I was the only non-drinker there. The social stigma of not drinking from a few years ago has mostly gone, and nobody seemed to care. Most people didn't even notice. It is becoming more and more common for people to stop drinking or at least reduce their alcohol consumption. Surveys suggest a third of 16- to 24-year-olds are now teetotal.

The first pub we went to had a selection of funky non-alcoholic craft beers, and the beer I had was indistinguishable from alcoholic beer. The second pub only had bottles of generic alcohol-free lager, and with a selection of very appealing alcoholic beers on tap, I did feel like I was missing out. One of the players was disappointed in me and kept trying to buy me a proper pint and then wanted me to do shots of tequila with him. I confess, I was a little tempted. But I resisted and he soon got bored. The social pressure to drink is no longer as strong as it once was and if I continue this alcohol-free experiment any longer, I don't think peer pressure would be a barrier.

But I have only been out four times in two months, so it's not been too much of a stretch.

The Self-Publishing Show

The toughest moment so far was at the Self-Publishing Show that I wrote about here. There was a free bar all night at the post-show social event. I arrived at the venue to find rows of glasses of red and white wine and buckets of ice-cold lager and pale ale. I asked the barman if they had any non-alcoholic beers.

'Sure,' he said, grabbing a bottle from the fridge behind him. 'That will be £6.50, please.'

'Oh, are they not included in the free drinks?'

'Unfortunately not. We've got jugs of water and some elderflower cordial for the non-drinkers.'

I declined the non-alcoholic beer and drank water for the rest of the night instead, while those around me drank a never-ending stream of beers and glasses of wine. That felt tough. Not because I wanted the beer or wine (I sort of did), but because they were getting exciting drinks for free, and I felt I was missing out.

Discovering Non-Alcoholic Beers

Non-alcoholic beers have been around for decades, but they've always been a bit crap – too sweet and too watery. Removing the alcohol also seemed to remove most of the flavour.

Things have changed dramatically, and not only are all the major brands and breweries releasing non-alcoholic versions of their popular drinks, but brewers who exclusively make non-alcoholic beers are springing up all the time. I have enjoyed the novelty of sampling different non-alcoholic beers and found some absolute belters.

My personal favourites so far are *Run Wild* by Athletic Brewing, all of the Big Drop Brewing beers (especially *Poolside IPA*), and the amazing, but expensive, *Little Wave* and *Shorebreak* from Firebrand Brewing. I could happily drink these instead of real beer forever.

Health Benefits?

The only positive I can take from the experiment so far is that it surely must be good for my health. I don't feel any better, but presumably my body is thanking me inside. Surely? To make it a more accurate and interesting experiment, I should have recorded some of my medical markers beforehand to compare. Things like blood pressure and, er, actually blood pressure is all I can think of.

Rachel's Decision

To complicate things further, Rachel stopped drinking just after I did. She drinks less than me at home, but more if we're out. She too is yet to experience any of the benefits of going alcohol-free.

If you've read any of my books (especially the *DNF Series*), you'll know that Rachel and I can get quite competitive with each other. Two months in, there is no way she will go back to alcohol if I am still abstaining. If I start drinking again, however, I'm fairly sure she will too. But she'll wait for me to be the one to start first so that she can claim the moral victory. You're not getting a medal, Rachel!

The Crossroads

I'm now at a crossroads.

Do I keep this alcohol-free experiment going in the hopes that one day soon I will wake up feeling like the changed man I thought I would? Do I hold out in the hope that suddenly it will all make sense? Or do I just crack open a beer now and celebrate my two months and the fact that at least I tried? It's a tough decision to make.

My relationship with alcohol has already changed. Hopefully for the better. And if I do go back to drinking, I like to think I'll be better at moderating it. There's always the option of becoming a social drinker and only drinking when I'm out or have friends over (which is almost never anyway). I honestly don't know how long I will stick at it. I keep reminding myself that in a week, month, or year, am I likely to regret taking a break from alcohol? It's very unlikely.

For now, I'll keep it going a little longer and see what happens. We're off camping for a few days next week, and there's nothing like sitting around the campfire late at night with a glass of red wine in hand. Sadly, I'm yet to find any alcohol-free red wine that comes even close to the real thing.

Your Thoughts?

Have you ever taken a break from alcohol? How did it go for you? Did you notice any significant changes or benefits? Or maybe you were considering it but I've now put you off. I'd love to hear your thoughts and experiences.

Me (sober) after England's defeat to Spain in the Euros. Face painting by Kitty.

In It for the Long Run

A 20th Wedding Anniversary Marathon

Last month, Rachel and I celebrated our 20th wedding anniversary. I say 'celebrated', but that's quite a loose definition of the word. Rachel is notoriously bad at remembering our anniversary and has forgotten almost half of them over the past 20 years. The rest she remembered thanks only to last-minute reminders from friends or family, so our celebrations are always very low key.

This year, we both remembered, and it seemed fitting to mark the occasion by running July's marathon together as part of our marathon-a-month challenge. Nothing says 'happy anniversary' like voluntarily running 26.2 miles together.

Our alarms went off at 5.15 am and after a quick breakfast of cereal, toast and tea, we were out of the door by 5.40 am.

The run didn't get off to the best of starts. Rachel was in tears at the top of the first hill, less than a mile from home.

'What's up?' I asked.

'I don't know. I think I'm just feeling a bit rubbish and not looking forward to the prospect of a marathon.'

'We don't have to do it today. It's not too late to turn back.'

'It's ok,' she sobbed. 'I'm fine.'

'You don't seem fine. Why don't we go home? There's plenty of time left in the month to do a marathon another day.'

'It's fine. Hopefully I'll feel better soon.'

The fear that her tears were somehow about our 20-year marriage rather than the run crept in. Here we were, with our anniversary marathon barely even started, and Rachel was already in tears. I couldn't help but wonder if she was upset about more than just the run.

'Are you sad because you've realised you've been married to me for 20 years?' I asked.

'No, of course not,' she sniffed.

It was dark and gloomy and the prospect of running 26.2 miles was not particularly appealing to me either. Part of me felt like crying too.

'Happy anniversary!' I said sarcastically.

Rachel gave an attempt at a laugh, but it wasn't very convincing.

Things improved slightly once the sun made an appearance. Everything feels better when the sun shines.

It's quite rare for me to see the sunrise during the summer months, but when I do get up early enough to witness it, it feels like a real privilege. My body didn't yet agree and still felt like it would rather be in bed. I always feel like that when I run first thing in the morning, but I know from experience that the feeling eases. Rachel, on the other hand, is able to bounce out of bed and begin running without issue. That's why it was so strange to see her out of sorts.

We followed bridleways and back roads from our house out towards the coast, which we met after seven miles without passing another person. It was 7 am and already swelteringly hot. There was a strong temptation for a swim, but we knew there would be plenty more opportunities during the day so pressed on.

I have run this stretch of the South West Coast Path many times before in every conceivable weather condition. I thought back to my first ever ultramarathon, featured in my book *Chasing Trails,* which took place along this coastline. We battled torrential rain, hail and 60mph winds, and I felt grateful that today's conditions were so favourable.

Being married for 20 years, Rachel and I value our own space and knew we didn't need to fill all 26.2 miles with chat. For large chunks of the marathon, we both had our headphones in. Often, when out running together, we'll listen to the same podcast at the same time, so while we are in our own worlds, we are also having a shared experience.

There was lots of time without our headphones too. We reminisced about our wedding day and everything that has happened in those 20 years since. Three children, several career changes, relocating our family to Devon, adventures had together, countless happy memories formed, and plenty of challenges overcome.

After about 11 miles we stopped for a swim in a stunning, secluded cove.

'Where is everyone?' said Rachel. 'It's the middle of July!'

'It's also 8.15 am on a Wednesday. I think people are getting ready for school or work.'

'8.15 am? I thought it was lunchtime. I'm so hungry.'

'Me too.'

A makeshift picnic of cheese sandwiches and crisps (salt and vinegar Hula Hoops, of course) helped refuel us for the rest of the run.

'Sorry about being so emotional earlier,' she said.

'That's ok. Are you feeling better?'

'Much. Thank you. I don't know what was wrong with me. I just wasn't feeling it earlier.'

'Are you sure it wasn't sadness about being married to me for 20 years?'

She laughed again. This time is sounded slightly more convincing.

It always strikes me as odd that running for many miles along hilly terrain can have a positive effect on your state of mind. Everything about running suggests it should make things worse, but it does have a strange transformative effect. Rachel's tears earlier weren't about us after all (at least, I hope they weren't), they were just part of the process, part of the release that running often brings.

Knowing that we would be gone for a long time, we had set off early so that we were home in time to collect the children from school. This meant that they would have to get themselves up and sorted in the morning.

It was the final week of term and, instead of the usual lessons, the school put on various activities for the children. Kitty was due to take part in a day's cookery tutorial but had been reluctant to go in because her best friend was no longer going. We told her she couldn't stay home alone and had to go in.

With no phone signal for two hours along this remote stretch of coastline we had to trust that everything was ok.

When our phones finally got back into range, we discovered 81 messages in our family WhatsApp group. Kitty had reluctantly gone to school but was very upset and cross that there was nobody she knew doing the day's cookery activity.

She had sent us dozens of messages asking if she could go home.

Layla and Leo had shown their usual lack of compassion, with a series of messages to Kitty.

Leo: *Stop moaning. Idiot.*

Layla: *Pathetic. Just do cooking.*

As we scrolled through the messages, it seemed that things had quickly escalated. One of Kitty's teachers had then seen her looking upset so suggested she join a different group who were getting a bus to do a high-ropes course in another town. But she needed parental consent to be able to take part. And Kitty's useless parents were out running a marathon and uncontactable.

Leo, finally deciding to be helpful, had replied: *Hi. Mum here. I consent.*

Kitty replied: *Nice try Leo. It needs to be verbal. And from an actual parent.*

Fortunately, Kitty had been allowed to board the bus and by the time we called her, they had not arrived at the destination so we were able to give our consent for her to take part in the day's activity.

Rachel and I felt terrible for being lousy parents but were relieved Kitty was now doing an activity she was excited about with a group of friends she liked.

We couldn't resist a second swim at a beach at 18 miles, and more sandwiches and crisps.

Leaving the coast after about 20 miles, we ventured back inland and arrived home six and a half hours after we started.

There are lots of similarities that can be drawn between marriage and marathon running.

They are a commitment and need patience and perseverance. Both require us to be there for each other, especially during the tough times. There are highs and lows, moments of elation and periods of utter exhaustion. Discomfort and tears (and chafing) are part of the journey. There are times you want to give up. Not all of it is fun. Or easy. But the rewards make it all worthwhile, and, despite the challenges, there are no regrets about stepping over that start line. We are in it for the long run.

I'm looking forward to many more years of marriage. I hope Rachel is too. Some might argue that a nice meal out would have been a better way to celebrate a wedding anniversary, but I think our marathon was perfectly fitting and certainly memorable. Perhaps it will become a new annual tradition? That's if Rachel remembers.

There will come a time when we look back fondly and think: *'Remember that time we ran a marathon on our wedding anniversary?'* But I hope we still have many more years to create these memories.

Welly Wanging, Waterfalls, and Wayward Golf Balls

If the purpose of a holiday is to relax, refresh, and rejuvenate, then the week's break we've just returned from was a spectacular failure.

My family and I, along with my parents, sister, and her family, spent a week in North Devon. It was one of the most exhausting weeks of my life, where we crammed what felt like a month's worth of activities into seven frenetic days.

We were staying at a place called Manor & Ashbury near Okehampton, which is a sports, leisure and crafts resort. There's a full timetable of various activities scheduled each day all included in the cost of your stay, and you sign up to any that take your fancy. One minute you might be playing dodgeball, the next you're making a felt frog. Then you're doing a spot of pistol shooting, before squeezing in an ice curling tournament – all before lunch.

Activities are booked via sheets of paper pinned to the wall in the bookings room. There is talk of them releasing an app, but I hope they don't. There's something satisfyingly old-school about scrawling your name onto a list with a pencil.

With 12 of us in our group, Rachel, my mum, and my sister took the lead in booking activities. And I spent the week being told what I was doing and when. I often wouldn't get informed until the very last minute via a family text.

'GEORGE, WHERE ARE YOU? The climbing wall session starts in FIVE MINUTES!!!'

'On my way! Just finished aqua zumba.'

The staff were all very relaxed and amenable, and people were allowed to come and go as they pleased. The woman who led the Tai Chi class, however, didn't get this memo. Layla signed all 12 of us up to for a session one afternoon.

Before the class began, I politely told the instructor that four of us would have to leave ten minutes early to get to a badminton tournament, and I expected her to say that it was absolutely fine. Instead, she just gave me an ice-cold glare and asked where the tournament was taking place. I explained that it was on the other side of the resort.

'Well, that's not ideal, is it?' she said, not breaking eye contact. 'But it is what it is. You'll miss the best bit.'

I thought I had managed to win her over slightly with a reference to *Karate's Kid*'s 'wax on, wax off' during one of the moves we learned, but her smile quickly faded. She then explained to the group that Tai Chi is a moving meditation but also a martial art, and while she used me as a prop to demonstrate one of the moves, I genuinely thought she was going to body slam me into the floor.

We escaped just in time to join the badminton tournament, only to hear later that my nephew had vomited all over the Tai Chi room floor soon after we left. Karma, perhaps?

The sports are open to all ages and abilities. One minute you might be paired against a couple of ex-professionals, then next your opposition is a five-year-old child playing with a grandparent on crutches.

There's something about that place that stirs up an intensely competitive spirit – mostly because of the £5 gift shop voucher given to the winner of each activity. By the end of the week, we had won enough competitions between us for us each to get a T-shirt from the gift shop.

Leo and Layla proved an impressive badminton pair and made it to three semi-finals. Kitty and I were less successful, and Kitty rued her choice of partner. She was furious with me because I let a six-year-old take some of his serves again and hit a few of his shots that were sailing well outside the court. They went on to beat us when I mistakenly got the scoring wrong.

'What did you do that for?' she hissed, after we had shaken hands with the victors. 'You didn't even try to hit that last one over the net.'

'I'm sorry, I thought we were playing to 21. Not 11. I thought we had loads of time left to win.'

Leo and Layla's winning streak came to an end when they were thoroughly thrashed on the badminton court in the semi-final by an eight-year-old prodigy and his dad. Seeking revenge, Leo and I faced the same pair in a pickleball competition the next day and emerged victorious. We then got annihilated in the next match by a married couple in their late seventies.

Mealtimes were a strange affair. You'd be standing in line for the buffet, trying to recall if the person next to you was the one who kicked your ass at bowls or the father of the boy who you nearly drowned during water polo. Sometimes, it turned out to be both. Conversations were polite and courteous, but there was always a fierce undercurrent of competition simmering just below the surface, ready to boil over as soon as the next activity began.

Throughout the week, we also took part in badminton, football, padel, tennis, bowls, table bowls, target bowls, ice curling, new kurling, archery, pistol shooting, welly wanging, rifle shooting, pool, snooker, skittles, Mario Kart Grand Prix, rounders, continuous cricket and bingo. There's also an extensive craft centre with dozens of different classes each day. Layla and Kitty did some Indian block printing and pottery transfers, but Rachel, Leo, and I were too fully booked with other sporting activities to have time for crafting.

During the occasional break between activities, we would usually end up in the swimming pool. After a few hours of being demolished in various activities, I'd often slink off to the sauna, hoping for some peace and quiet. Of course, on this holiday, relaxation was never allowed to be relaxing.

Leo, Kitty and my niece and nephews would soon join me in the sauna, and then proceed to spoon ladle after ladle of water onto the hot coals until the temperature reached furnace levels. They would then immediately evacuate the sauna and leave me there to cook. It got so hot that I couldn't take in air because my throat and lungs were being scorched. Saunas are supposed to be good for you, but I'm not sure the experience is quite as beneficial when your eyeballs begin to melt.

My mum optimistically took three books with her. She had six pages left in one book and two new ones to start. By the end of the week, she'd only managed to finish those six pages. My book never made it out of my bag.

Before we had kids, Rachel and I would occasionally play pitch and putt. The very first time we played together, we stood on the tee of a short 70-yard hole. I went first, hitting the ball poorly, but somehow it shot down the fairway like a rocket, scooted across the green, slammed into the flag, and dropped straight into the hole.

'Oh my God!!' I shouted. 'A hole in one!'

Rachel just stood there, completely unimpressed.

'Rachel? Did you see that? I just got a hole-in-one. It went in the hole. IN ONE!'

'Isn't that what you're supposed to do?' she replied, with zero enthusiasm.

I stared at her, dumbfounded.

'Well, yes, that's the goal, but it almost never happens!'

'Oh. Well, it did happen. Well done, you!'

I could have been playing golf with anyone else in the world, and they would have shown more excitement than Rachel did. It was possibly the most anticlimactic hole-in-one ever. I've never come close to another one since.

Fast forward to this holiday, and Rachel, Leo, my dad, and I decided to tackle a par-3 course one afternoon. My dad is a regular golfer, I play maybe once or twice a year, Rachel hadn't touched a club since those pitch and putt days nearly 20 years ago, and Leo was a complete beginner. Despite the odds, both Rachel and Leo did surprisingly well. Leo enjoyed it initially but grew frustrated as the game went on. Rachel, however, found her groove, and as her golf improved, so did her enjoyment.

Our final hole presented the biggest challenge: a lake cutting across the middle of the fairway. To clear the water, you needed to hit the ball about 100 yards. The furthest Rachel or Leo had managed was about 50 yards.

'Maybe you should play it safe and take a shorter shot, then try to clear the lake with your second one,' I suggested.

'No, don't be silly,' Rachel said, determined. 'I'm going for it.'

'That's the spirit!'

Rachel lined up her shot, and to my amazement, hit her best ball of the day. It sailed high into the air... and then plopped straight down into the lake. Leo followed suit with an identical result.

'Great effort, both of you. Those would've been fantastic shots... if only the lake wasn't in the way.'

I overcompensated, sending my ball way over the green, but at least it was safe and dry.

'What happens now?' asked Rachel.

'Well, technically, you should take a penalty drop by the water and try again to clear the lake. But if you want, you could just take your next shot on the green.'

'No chance. I want to do it properly. I'm going over the lake,' said Rachel.

'Me too!' said Leo.

They both took their second shots from down by the lake, and both promptly sent them straight into the water. Then the next ones. And the next. Fortunately, I had a big stash of old golf balls in my bag and was more than happy to lighten the load.

'Shall we call it a day?' I suggested as yet another ball splashed into the lake.

'One more,' said Rachel. 'Pleeease!'

'Fine, one more,' I said, handing over another ball.

It too ended up in the lake. So did Leo's.

'One more!' Rachel pleaded. 'Pleeeeease. Last one. I promise.'

'You said that for the last five!'

'I mean it this time. Pleeeaassse.'

'Alright! Last one!' I said, feeling like I was negotiating with toddlers.

Finally, their perseverance paid off, and they both managed to clear the lake with their final shots (although I'm certain there would have been yet another 'final shot' if they hadn't). Between them, they lost 14 balls on that hole, leaving my bag considerably lighter.

Ironically, when I took my second shot from the back of the green, I hit it way too hard, and it rolled right across the green and into the same bloody lake.

Make that 15 balls.

The day's activities didn't begin until 9 am, so we could have had a nice relaxing lie-in before breakfast.

But that was never going to happen.

On three mornings I went for a bike ride with Leo, Rachel, my dad and sister. Three mornings I went for a walk, and another I played golf with my mum and dad.

The mighty Yes Tor, the second-highest peak south of the Peak District (surpassed only by the nearby High Willhays), looms ominously in the distance above the hotel.

Very early one morning, Rachel, Layla and I decided to try and conquer it before breakfast.

We parked the car at Meldon Reservoir, a 10-minute drive from the hotel, and began our walk at 5.30 am. Following an established track around to the east, we gradually made our ascent.

We were treated to a stunning sunrise as it emerged from behind the hillside to our left. The early start had been worth it, long before we'd even reached the top.

The path soon faded, leaving us to forge our own way across rocks and tussocky marshland for the final half mile to the summit.

Just as we neared the top, a thick cloud enveloped us. The temperature dropped and visibility vanished. It was another reminder of Dartmoor's wild and untamed nature. Unsurprisingly, climbing Yes Tor is not a popular pre-breakfast activity, and we didn't encounter another soul during our two miles up and two miles down. We made it back to the hotel just in time for breakfast.

One afternoon, when we were taking a break from the scheduled activities, I suggested a walk to a 20-foot waterfall I had read about, located up a river near a viaduct in Okehampton. Two miles into the walk, I was confused about the lack of waterfall. It turns out I had not only started our walk from the wrong viaduct, but we had been following the wrong river entirely. I've now learned the difference between the West Okement and East Okement rivers.

Still, it was a very enjoyable walk and nobody seemed to mind too much that the promised waterfall didn't exist.

Determined to make amends, before breakfast on the final morning, Rachel, my mum, dad, Layla and I drove to the correct viaduct, found the correct river and walked and found the actual waterfall, and had an enjoyable – but painfully freezing – swim in a pool above it. The rest of the family, understandably, chose not to trust my navigation skills a second time.

Despite the multitude of activities on offer, it was these excursions outside of the resort that I enjoyed the most during the week. Give me a whole timetable of fun and exciting new sporting activities to try and I will be extremely happy. But give me a big hill, a woodland, or a river and I'll be even happier.

Not exhausted enough with her days full of activity, Rachel completed her August marathon early one morning. Setting off before sunrise, she was home in time for the morning's ice curling competition. I'll have to try and squeeze mine in later in the month.

A week feels like a very long time when almost every minute is filled with activity. As the new week at home began, I found myself adrift without a timetable dictating every moment of my day. The holiday, though exhausting, left me feeling like I had accomplished so much in such a short time, but back at home, I suddenly felt at a loss.

There's always plenty going on in my life, but I often spend more time thinking about what to do and deciding where to focus my energy than actually getting things done. Inspired by the holiday's rigid schedule, I'm going to start structuring my days better, blocking out time for each task in the hope of becoming more productive.

And who knows, I might even set aside some time for a bit of welly wanging.

THE DOG NEXT DOOR - PART TWO

AFTER A WEEK AWAY ON HOLIDAY, we returned home hopeful that the memory of the rook scarer – now over a month ago – had faded for Tan. Surely, all those positive memories from the hundreds of miles of happy walks we've had together would overwrite that one bad day.

Ludo came back from his week-long stay with our friends, and later that afternoon, I took him out for a walk. Tan was hanging out with Milo, our neighbour's Labrador, in their garden. I opened the gate, and Milo bounded up to me excitedly, knowing my presence meant a walk was imminent.

'Hi Tan,' I said, as enthusiastically as I could. 'Do you want to come for a walk?'

She walked over to me slowly, her head hung low, and then slipped past me as I stood in the gateway, back to her kennel in the yard.

I tried not to take it too personally.

The next morning, Layla took Ludo out for a walk, and Tan happily joined them, showing none of the suspicion she had toward me. I tried again later that afternoon, but she hid in her kennel once more.

Maybe a change of scene would help? We could try taking her to the beach? The mere suggestion of a car ride usually had her racing across the yard and leaping into the van, eager for an adventure.

But when I opened the van door and called her over, she just peeked out from her kennel before retreating further inside.

The next day, we tried a new, some might say deceptive, approach. I stayed inside while Layla opened the van door. Tan sprinted over and jumped straight onto the back seats. Layla doesn't drive, but Tan didn't know this. She just saw the opportunity to go somewhere fun (without me) and took it. I then casually climbed into the driver's seat and started the engine. Tan looked a little nervous and gave me the side-eye but didn't make a bid for freedom.

We made it to the beach, and suddenly, Tan was back to her old, happy self. This was progress! We had a couple more beach trips over the following week and each was a great success.

While we were trying to rebuild Tan's trust, our friends' dog Rufus, a young and dashing Labrador, came to stay with us for a week. He won 'Best in Show' at the local dog show, don't you know. Ludo's highest accolade is third place in the 'Dog Who Looks Most Like its Owner' category back in 2019.

Rufus was the perfect distraction for Tan. Suddenly, he was the focus of our walks and he flirted with Tan throughout the week, while I was reduced to a mere bystander.

But Tan had competition for Rufus's attention. He was also infatuated with Rose, the farm's ancient border collie. No one knows exactly how old Rose is, as she was inherited from another farm, who inherited her from another farm, handed down through different generations. She's basically a dog fossil – deaf, almost completely blind, and hobbles around the yard like every step might be her last.

But Rufus saw something special in Rose. He would disappear over our garden wall at every opportunity to spend quality time with her, and get to know Rose a bit better . And Rose, who usually staggers around like movement is a chore, couldn't get enough of it. She seemed to come alive when Rufus was around, skipping around the yard like she was ten years younger (Or 20? or 30? Who knows?), looking, with her very limited eyesight, for her toyboy.

We got home one day to find Rose on our doorstep, waiting for Rufus to be let out.

Tan enjoyed the extra company on our walks. With four dogs in tow, she regained her confidence. There were now sheep in the crop field where the rook scarer once stood, and sheep take precedence over everything for a border collie. She was back in stalking mode, with the rook scarer a distant memory.

We were almost back to how things were before the incident. Tan was excited to see me again and happy to go on walks – even the one where the rook scarer had once stood. But it seemed like she found safety in numbers, whether it was Rachel, Layla, or the presence of Rufus.

The final test was to see if she'd trust me alone.

This morning, I decided to try.

I took Ludo outside and called to Tan. Over the last few weeks, if I was on my own, Tan would have retreated to her kennel at this point. To my surprise, she ran straight over and began barking with excitement. The old Tan was back. I felt like I was finally forgiven.

We passed into the field, and the dogs raced ahead as usual. I noticed the latch staple that secures the gate lying on the ground. I pushed it with my thumb and then the palm of my hand into the holes of the gatepost, but it still felt a little wobbly. A big gust of wind or a nudge from a sheep or cow and it would pop straight out again. This was the main gate between the field and a road, so it was very important that it was always closed securely.

I picked up a nearby rock and gave the staple a few bashes to secure it in place. The noise of rock on metal echoed through the valley.

Like a gunshot.

WHAT WAS I THINKING?

Tan, who had been far off in the field, came running back at the sound. She ducked under the gate and stood in the road, looking back at me. I put the rock down immediately and called her back.

'It's ok, Tan. I was just fixing the gate. It's nothing to be scared of.'

She paused, looked at me suspiciously for a few seconds with that same expression from a few weeks ago, when her trust in me vanished. Then she turned for home.

I called after her, but she didn't return. When we got back from the walk, I found her sitting in her kennel.

And just like that, we're back to square one. This time it was down to my own stupidity. Every time she sees me now, her head drops, and she retreats to the safety of her kennel.

And I'll have to earn her trust all over again.

The Choosing

'Do you fancy going camping in Cornwall for a couple of nights next week?' said Rachel on the sofa one evening. 'I've found the perfect site. It's near to that beach I mentioned.'

'Yeah ok, sounds good. Let's book it.'

'Er... well you can't actually book it.'

'What do you do? Just turn up and hope they have a spot?'

'Well, sort of,' she said. 'It's very popular. You have to arrive at 8 am.'

'8 am? Isn't it about three hours away?'

'Yeah.'

'So if you turn up at 8 am then you're guaranteed to get a pitch, right?'

'No. That's when you register your interest to say you want a pitch.'

'You're joking? Register your interest? And then what happens?'

'When you've registered your interest, you go away and come back again at 10.30.'

'And then you get a pitch?'

'No, that's when you find out if you've been successful.'

'And if we don't get one?'

'We'll worry about that if it happens. I guess we could try to find another site. Or just come home again.'

'This sounds like the worst campsite ever.'

I did some googling and found another campsite nearby, equally close to the beach. It was cheaper, with free showers, Wi-Fi, and guaranteed bookings. But Rachel was fixated on the experience of this particular campsite, lured by the uncertainty of what I jokingly started calling 'The Choosing.'

The Choosing seemed to be part of the charm for Rachel. It turned what could have been a simple camping trip into a quest. I didn't get it, but Rachel did, and she wasn't going to be swayed by something as practical as online booking and guaranteed accommodation.

Layla decided not to join us. Driving to Cornwall and not having anywhere to stay didn't fill her with much excitement. But the best-case scenario – securing a pitch and spending two nights in a tent with her family – sounded even worse to her. So, she opted to stay at home and feed the cat instead.

Having loaded up the van the night before, we hit the road at 4.45 am. Leo and Kitty were surprisingly upbeat about heading off so early, reminding me of the thrill I used to feel on holidays as a kid. But those early starts would have been to catch a ferry, flight or begin a long drive to Devon or the Lake District, not for the opportunity to register our interest in a campsite that may or may not have availability.

It was a strange feeling driving to Cornwall – a mix of mild anxiety, and, I admit, a little excitement about the uncertainty of our adventure.

We parked in the village of Treen (you're not allowed to park in the campsite until you are 'chosen') and walked to Treen Farm Campsite, arriving at 7.55 am.

'Are those our ops?' said Leo, pointing to two people already lurking outside reception.

'Ops?' said Rachel.

'Yeah, ops. Our opposition. Our enemy,' he said.

'Yes, looks like they are,' I said. 'They are here for The Choosing too.'

'IT'S NOT CALLED THE CHOOSING!' laughed Rachel. 'STOP CALLING IT THAT!'

Others arrived minutes after us. I wanted to hate them – the other families (our ops), the staff, the whole process. I wanted the employees to be as annoying and pretentious as their stupid booking policy. I wanted to be able to smugly say to Rachel, 'See, I told you we should've just gone to the other site.'

But everyone was extremely lovely and welcoming, and the place did have a really nice laidback feel to it.

And why should the campsite take bookings? This was how campsites used to operate before the internet and before telephones. It's how this site had operated successfully for decades. Why did they need to change?

After 'registering our interest' with the campsite, we had two and half hours to kill until we discovered our fate at The Choosing.

The reason Rachel had been so desperate to visit this particular campsite was because of its proximity to a beach she had passed with a friend a couple of months ago – Pedn Vounder (we made a mess of it each time we tried to say it, but I think it's pronounced 'Pednee'). We headed down to check it out.

We had read online that accessing the beach was a little challenging and involved a steep descent. This was an understatement. It starts out steep and rocky and gets worse the further down the cliff it goes. The final 20 metres is a fairly terrifying, near vertical climb down the rock.

Ludo was with us, and it was difficult to know whether it was safer for him to find his own way down or keep him on his lead. We quickly realised he was far more adept than us at managing the terrain and would likely pull us over the edge if kept on his lead. We let him off and he was standing on the beach seconds later. It's possible he bounced the entire way down the cliff face, but he looked happy enough as he raced around the empty beach.

The rest of us were a little slower and more cautious with our descent.

'Right, it's time to get back for The Choosing,' I said, the moment we set foot on the sand.

'Are you serious?' said Kitty. 'We've only just got here.'

'No, I'm only joking. We've got loads of time. Who's coming for a swim?'

Rachel, Leo and Kitty looked out at the crashing waves and didn't respond.

'Oh, just me then.'

The waves were particularly brutal, and I spent 10 minutes in the sea getting an absolute beating. But it was great fun, and I felt very privileged to be enjoying this popular Cornish beauty spot so early in the morning.

The only other people on the beach were a couple and their young daughter who arrived a few minutes before us. The man had promptly stripped off all of his clothes and ran straight into the sea. He then spent a few minutes air drying his bits before running into the sea again. He made me feel very overdressed.

We spent an hour walking the beach, exploring the many caves, and watching several people descend the path to the beach and then chicken out at the final steep section and retreat back up the cliff. When we left the beach at 10 am, the naked man and his family were still the only other people there.

Arriving back at the campsite's reception, there were now about 10 different families and couples waiting for the 10.30 results of The Choosing.

'STOP CALLING IT THE CHOOSING!' said Rachel.

At 10.30 on the dot, one of the members of staff emerged from reception and read out a name. It was the couple who had arrived just before us – our ops.

'Come inside,' said the young member of staff, and the couple walked with her into reception where they would discover their fate.

Five minutes later they emerged looking victorious and followed the member of staff to their pitch.

'Are we next?' whispered Kitty.

'I hope so,' I said.

'Manchin? Er... Moorhen? Er... Meathouse?' called the woman, staring at a piece of paper and looking puzzled.

'Mahood?' Rachel offered.

'That sounds right,' she said. 'Thank you! Sorry we couldn't read our own writing.'

'Meathouse?' I sniggered quietly to myself as Rachel followed the woman into reception.

It was a long nervous wait, but Rachel emerged a few minutes later with a big smile across her face. She gave us a thumbs up.

We had been chosen.

We were shown to our spot, a large pitch bordered by a hedge, and I returned to the car park to get the van. An hour later, the tent was up, we were unpacked. And ready to properly begin our two-day holiday.

Pedn Vounder, which had been breathtaking on our early morning visit, was a different level of spectacular when we returned to it in the midday sun.

Once a remote cove known only to locals, Pedn Vounder has become increasingly popular with its stunning beauty being shared by newspapers, magazines, social media influencers and idiots writing books about it.

There was now a queue of people descending the treacherous path. But it's a big beach and there was plenty of room.

The naked man from earlier was still there, still naked, and completely unfazed by the dozens of people who had now joined him on the beach.

We spent a few hours swimming, digging holes, reading, playing bat and ball, and nervously watching others make their way down the path.

'This is the best beach I have ever been to,' said Kitty. Rachel and I couldn't disagree.

The beach was all the more desirable after the effort required to get there. I don't think it would have had the same appeal or charm had you been able to park right next to it.

Perhaps in the same way that the campsite was all the better after the challenge involved with getting a pitch. The reward was sweeter because we had to earn it.

That evening, we drove to Sennen Cove. Despite being on the north coast of Cornwall, it was only a ten-minute drive from the south. We watched the waves crash against the sea wall and ate fish and chips perched on a rock above the town.

With only two nights in Cornwall, we were determined to make the most of every minute. We returned to the campsite, and, while Leo and Kitty were done for the day, Rachel, Ludo, and I walked across the fields to a lookout above Porthcurno and watched a magnificent sunset.

I have been fairly obsessed with the South West Coast Path for many years. The 630-mile trail winds its way along the coastlines of Dorset, Devon, Cornwall and Somerset. Completing the entire thing one day is top of my bucket list. Thanks to various camping holidays in the South West, we've covered substantial portions of it over the years. Leo and Kitty knew that our two days in Cornwall would almost certainly involve some kind of walk along the coast.

Convincing the kids to tackle an out-and-back hike, however, is always a challenge. 'You mean we've got to walk this same way back? What's the POINT? Why don't we just turn around now?'
The alternative is to do a loop that returns via inland routes. While this gives the walk a bit more purpose and feels less repetitive, the second half is often more boring than the first, with sections across fields and along roads that can't quite compete with the cliffs and sea views.

But there was a third option.

One of us (most likely me) could drive the van ahead along the coast, then run back to the campsite, making the van the endpoint of our walk. This way, we could enjoy a full coastal route without the temptation to turn back halfway.

At 8.30 the following morning, I parked the van in the vast, but empty car park at Britain's most south-westerly point – Land's End.

This place held a special significance for me as it was the starting point of my penniless Land's End to John O'Groats trip all those years ago.

On my two previous visits, Land's End had been virtually deserted. The first time, Ben and I set off on our adventure in our boxer shorts on a cold, wet morning, with nobody around except a couple of Australian tourists. The second visit was during a family holiday to St Ives just before Christmas in 2018, and the place was similarly empty.

It's a large sprawling complex with gift shops, food outlets and a petting zoo. And on this occasion too, it was eerily deserted. I reminded myself that it was 8.30 am. Perhaps there would be a few more tourists when we returned to pick up the van later in the day. I couldn't help but wonder if the whole thing is a front for some money laundering operation as there seemed no possible way it was sustainable as a tourist attraction.

I ran the four miles back to the campsite along nice easy roads, knowing the coastal route we would follow for the walk would be much further and a lot more challenging.

A very welcome coffee and bacon-and-egg roll awaited me on my return, and after a quick shower, we were ready to begin our walk. It turns out Kitty's trainers were in the van that I had parked at Land's End, so she had to tackle the seven-mile walk in a pair of Crocs. Leo was opting to wear Crocs anyway.

The coast path dropped down into the picturesque village of Porthcurno. Many of the beaches along this stretch of coast featured in the hit TV drama *Poldark* (I haven't seen it), but it is understandable why it was chosen as a cinematic backdrop.

The path climbed steeply from the beach up past the glorious open-air Minack Theatre. With its stone terraces carved into the cliffs and sweeping ocean views, it resembles an ancient Greek amphitheatre, though it's surprisingly modern, having been built in 1930.

We continued down into the charming cove of Porthchapel and then onto Porthgwarra, where we bought pasties for lunch later on.

The path was flanked by stunning purple heather and bright yellow gorse and we stopped at the spectacular, but weirdly named, Nanjizal beach to eat our pasties. We had a fun swim in the Song of the Sea Cave – a turquoise tidal pool that sits beneath a giant rock arch. It was an exciting and novel change from our usual sea swims.

Half an hour later, after a walk of seven miles, we crested the headland and caught sight of Land's End. But something was different. There were other people there. Not just a couple of lost tourists. Hundreds of them. The place was packed.

It seems Land's End is a popular destination after all. Just not, understandably, on the early mornings of my previous visits, or the middle of December. The queue of people waiting to pay for a photograph by the iconic sign stretched for nearly 100 metres, hordes of people swarmed the food outlets, the gift shop was bustling, and the sprawling car park was full to the brim.

'What is this place?' said Kitty.

'Why is everyone here?' asked Leo.

'I've no idea,' I said.

We bought an ice cream and made our escape.

That evening, hoping to enjoy another sunset experience, Rachel, Ludo and I turned left on the coast path and walked in the opposite direction from the previous evening, this time out towards Logan Rock.

We thought that the entire promontory that sits high above the eastern edge of Pedn Vounder was called Logan Rock. But it turns out Logan Rock is an actual rock.

It's an example of a rocking stone and, despite weighing 80 tons, can supposedly be rocked by hand. Back in April 1824, Lieutenant Hugh Goldsmith and a team of his naval seamen colleagues, set out to disprove the claim that the rock could not be toppled. Armed with iron bars, Goldsmith and his men decided to prove how tough the navy was and pushed Logan Rock from its perch.

The locals were outraged. The rock was loved by all those who knew it and had also proved popular in bringing tourists to the area. Thankfully, the boulder had not fallen all the way into the sea and Goldsmith was ordered by the Admiralty to replace the stone to its former position and to try to undo some of the damage that had been done. It took many months, and a complex scaffolding and winch system to get the boulder back into place. But they successfully achieved their goal, and Goldsmith gained back some forgiveness from the people of Cornwall.

Rachel and I didn't make it up to the actual boulder. A heavy storm was forecast and the wind had picked up dramatically, making climbing around on the rock stacks seem a little unwise.

Back at the campsite, I tightened our tent's guy ropes and moved the van to help act as a wind break. I'm not sure it made much difference.

Our tent shook violently all night and the rain battered the canvas. At 2 am I could hear tent pegs being frantically hammered into the ground of a neighbouring tent. I don't think I got more than an hour's sleep combined all night, as I lay there waiting for ours to take off.

It sounded like the rain had stopped when we eventually crawled out of our sleeping bags, but when I stepped outside, the air was thick with moisture – somehow it was almost wetter than if it had been raining. There was no chance the tent would be dry before the strict 10 am departure.

We began packing away and stuffed everything into the van wet knowing we (I) would have to get it all out again once we got home.

Was it really worth it? To drive all that way with no guarantee of getting anywhere to stay? Then stay for just two nights and have to drive home and unpack the tent again? Really? Would we do it again?

Absolutely.

Rachel had been right. The Choosing ('STOP CALLING IT THAT!') was not an inconvenience after all. It was part of the adventure. That initial uncertainty had given the experience a heightened sense of appreciation.

And if we hadn't got a pitch? Then we would have made a new plan, which would have unfolded in a different way. It's all about embracing the unknown and trying to find some joy in the journey, whichever way it leads.

The Hornet Dilemma

'KILL THEM, LUDO! KILL THEM! KILL THEM, LUDO! KILL THEM!'

It was a disconcerting series of shouts to be woken to in the middle of the night.

'KILL THEM, LUDO! KILL THEM! GO ON, LUDO! QUICKLY! KILL THEM!'

I knew immediately that the voice was our 12-year-old daughter Kitty's, but I didn't know what or whom she was instructing our dog Ludo to kill.

Rachel stirred slightly but rolled over and went back to sleep. She used to have an almost supernatural ability to hear even the slightest murmur from the children when they were babies and she would be up and out of bed in seconds. Now they are older and much less dependent on her, Rachel has developed the opposite skill: an almost supernatural ability to tune them out completely.

I got out of bed and walked down the corridor to Kitty's room. She was sitting on the bed with a duvet over her head, while Ludo raced around the room barking angrily at two hornets that were buzzing at the lightbulb.

Hornets are rarely seen where we live, but this summer has been very different.

From about May onwards, we started seeing hornets regularly in our garden. It was usually only one at a time, so we did wonder for a while if it was perhaps the same hornet that just enjoyed hanging out at our house. Did we have a new pet?

We then started seeing multiple hornets in our house, particularly late in the evening, when they would fly in through the open windows, attracted by the light. Their rapid increase in numbers over the following days led us to believe there was a nest nearby.

Back in Kitty's bedroom, I managed to shoo one of the hornets back out the skylight from where it came. The second one I trapped in a glass, slipping a piece of paper under it and releasing it out of the window. With the hornets back outside and the skylight closed, Kitty emerged from under her duvet, and I said goodnight again.

The following night, a particularly determined hornet made its way into Leo's room just as I was heading to bed.

'GEORGE!' shouted Leo. 'HORNET!'

Last Christmas, Leo, now 14, was about an inch shorter than me. By Easter, he was an inch taller. And he likes to regularly remind me of this as he stands on tiptoes in the kitchen looking down on me. He's also declared himself 'the man of the house'. This doesn't apply to hornets, apparently. Or spiders. Or doing anything useful around the house. It seems just to be an accolade he has awarded himself for being the tallest.

The hornet had flown down the back of Leo's computer desk and the gap was too tight for me to fit a glass behind. It kept buzzing up the wall, almost to the top of the desk, and then would drop back down. I spent nearly ten minutes waiting for it to get high enough for me to catch it. Eventually it crested above the top of the desk, and I placed a glass over it. Heading over to the open window, I stuck my arm outside, removed the piece of paper and gave the glass a little shake. The hornet flew out of the glass, straight back over my shoulder and resumed its place behind Leo's desk.

It was another ten minutes before I caught it again. This time I took it outside the front door before releasing it.

Layla and I went away for a couple of nights in early August, and it all kicked off in our family group chat.

> *Rachel: Three hornets in kitty's bedroom. She is sleeping in the lounge.*
> *Rachel: OMG there's hornets everywhere. Coming in bathroom skylight. I can't leave my room.*
> *Leo: The man of the house has stepped down. Dord we need you. I'm not worthy of this job.*
> *Rachel: I've stepped down too. I'm a prisoner in my own room.*
> *Rachel: We're all wimps. All I can hear is buzzing.*

I replied, trying to reassure them the hornets were fine.

> *Don't be afraid of them. They are very docile.*

There were a couple more messages from Rachel the following morning.

> *Rachel: I'm going out there. Wish me luck.*

And then a few minutes later…

Rachel: We appear to be HORNET FREE, I repeat HORNET FREE. Free movement through the house once again permitted.

We found the nest a few days later. It was just four paces from our house, cleverly wedged between the back of an open stable door and the wall of a wooden shed. I had never seen a hornets' nest up close before, and it was a work of art – beautifully crafted but resembling something from *Alien*.

Hornets have a bad reputation and a lot of it is unjust. It's mostly due to their Asian counterparts and the sensationlised headlines every year from the British press.

KILLER HORNETS SET TO DECIMATE THE UK!
SWARMS OF HORNETS ON THE RAMPAGE!
HORNET ARMAGEDDON IS HERE!

While the invasive Asian hornets can be extremely destructive to bee colonies, the European hornets are misunderstood. They are big and noisy and pretty scary looking. But they are also very docile, non-aggressive and play an important ecological role as pollinators and pest controllers.

Only female hornets sting. I didn't realise that this is also the same with wasps and bees. I don't know about you, but determining the sex of insects is not my strong point, so I tend not to take my chances.

Despite not being as dangerous as first feared, hornets are still intimidating. I remember being dive-bombed by a May bug in the middle of the night a few years ago. The May bug, also known as a cockchafer, is big, noisy, clumsy and completely harmless. But when you have one buzzing around your head in the middle of the night it is pretty terrifying. Nobody wants a cockchafer in the bedroom.

The typical reaction when we encounter nature in our own homes is to exterminate it. We bring out the mouse traps, the fly spray, the wasp traps and we call in the pest controllers. We dig up the weeds, poison those slugs and stop the birds from shitting all over our cars. It's become a human instinct to assert control over nature and try to tame it. By doing this we create an imaginary divide between us and the rest of the natural world, forgetting the fact that we are part of nature.

Our first thought on discovering the hornets' nest was to work out a way to get rid of it.

Surely, we can't live with a hornets' nest four paces from our door?

We then discovered that unlike with bees, pest controllers don't 'rehome' hornets. They would just be gassed and killed, which seemed harsh. If they had built their nest in our lounge or kitchen, we would have felt differently. But they had picked a disused shed on the farm and were just a small inconvenience, rather than a hazard.

They aren't malicious and they are just doing what hornets do. I'm not entirely sure what it is they do exactly, but they look very industrious and are always busy. Hornets are just trying to get by in the world, just like the rest of us.

So we have decided to leave them.

It's been quite refreshing to just accept that they are there and that we've got to deal with them being there, rather than having them 'dealt with'.

Not everyone in our household shares this newfound philosophy of peaceful coexistence. Rachel is fully on board. Layla, Leo and Kitty seem ok with the arrangement, now that they've learned to keep their windows closed in the evenings. The only one of us who is not happy is Ludo. It probably wasn't helped with Kitty riling him up and instructing him to 'KILL THEM, LUDO! KILL THEM!' but he hates them more than I've seen him hate anything ever before. With the exception of drones. There was a drone that buzzed over us unexpectedly on Dartmoor once, and Ludo tried to take it out of the sky. Perhaps that's why he hates hornets so much. To him, they are basically little drones.

When he hears one buzz or sees one fly past, he leaps into action as the self-declared hornet exterminator. He jumps up at them, teeth gnashing and barking manically.

Despite this, they have shown no signs of aggression towards us or Ludo. Ludo had been all bark and no bite until one evening last week. The door to our garden is mostly glass and the hornets bounce against it at night when the lights are on in the kitchen and it's dark outside. I let Ludo out to go to the toilet before I went to bed, and he got angry with one of these hornets buzzing on the windowpane. He lunged at it mouth first and then suddenly dashed inside, his eyes comically wide and bulging. He then began licking his lips frantically while the hornet he had tried to eat staggered clumsily on the floor.

Ludo quickly learned his lesson. He still hates them. Still barks at them. He even gets cross now if we mention the word 'hornet'. But since being stung in the mouth, he no longer tries to eat them. He too is learning (the hard way) how to live with nature.

You might be thinking the whole family has reached some sort of zen-like state with the hornets and that we now sit calmly and eat dinner with them buzzing around the room and resting on our dinner plates. That's not quite the harmonious co-living we have cultivated. There is still a great deal of shrieking, flailing, slamming of doors and hiding under duvets whenever one gets inside.

But leaving the hornets alone has been a good lesson in learning to coexist better with nature. We all share this planet, and it is much healthier for us to view ourselves as actively part of nature, rather than the evil overlords that we too often are.

In my book, *The Self-Help Bible*, I wrote about nature's important role in our lives, though I also added a caveat for mosquitoes, fleas, and ticks: '*they can all fuck right off.*' I stand by that. I'm sure mosquitoes, fleas, and ticks all serve some valuable purpose in the ecosystem, but I don't want them anywhere near mine. I think it's very unlikely I'll ever feel a desire to coexist with them.

Hornets, however, I've found that I am not only tolerant of, but I also actually quite like them being there. I enjoy seeing them hard at work, doing whatever it is that they do, creating this magnificent home for themselves out of wood fibre and saliva, when I struggle to put together flat-pack furniture from IKEA.

They should move on in the autumn. And when I say, 'move on', I don't mean to a new home. I mean to that big hornet's nest in the sky. Sadly, only the queen will survive the winter and so the rest of the colony will die off in the next few months. I think I might actually miss them.

Until then, we'll continue to respect their space and hope that they try to respect ours. It's funny to think about how we've gone from shouting for Ludo to 'KILL THEM' to accepting their presence as part of our daily lives. And the hornets have taught us that we can just about live peacefully together.

So long as we don't try to eat them.

THE DOG NEXT DOOR - PART THREE

SINCE THE INCIDENT WITH the rook scarer in *The Dog Next Door: Part One,* and my subsequent stupidity in **Part Two**, I've been working hard to rebuild Tan's trust. But despite my best efforts, she still refuses to come out for walks with me from home, even though she's perfectly happy to trot along with Layla or our neighbours. It's only me she distrusts.

We've continued taking Tan with us on trips to the beach, and she's looking more and more at home during our family adventures. It still requires someone else to open the van door and encourage her in, though – if I am the instigator, she bolts back to her kennel. Layla and I recently managed a six-mile walk home from the beach with Tan and Ludo and she seemed genuinely happy and relaxed in my company.

Because these trips are much longer than Tan's usual walks, we've created a makeshift *'Back Soon'* sign which we hang on her kennel whenever we take her out. It's simple, but it reassures everyone that she's safe and sound.

One evening last week, Layla and I took Ludo and Tan up a nearby hill to watch the sunset. It's pretty rare for me to sit still on the ground for any length of time during our dog walks, so while I was on the grass enjoying the sky, Tan rushed over to me, a little confused – maybe even concerned – that I was sitting down and not moving. She licked my face as if to check that everything was alright. I gave her a lot of love and affection and she pawed at my chest, wanting more attention.

For a brief, glorious moment, it felt like the heart-stirring climax of a Hollywood epic. Cue the sweeping orchestral soundtrack, the soft-focus filter capturing Tan and me running through sun-dappled fields in slow motion. Fireworks bursting dramatically behind us (actually, given Tan's history with loud noises, scrap that stupid idea). And there's Ludo, always wanting to be the main character, nipping at my heels to make sure I hadn't forgotten him.

Had I finally been forgiven?

I didn't want to rush things, and didn't want to assume Tan was ready to walk with me unaccompanied, so I set off again the following day with Layla as a chaperone.

After stepping through the first gate, less than a hundred metres from home, we noticed Tan was limping. I walked up to her and she allowed me to lift up her leg and examine her paw. I found a thorn protruding from one of the pads and I removed the offending item. She put her foot down, squealed with excitement, and nuzzled up to my leg as if to say, 'Thank you.' I was quietly overjoyed, thinking this was another hugely significant step. I even melodramatically decided that the thorn wasn't just physical; maybe it symbolised the barriers that had been between us lately. She raced up the hill into the field with Ludo and Milo and it felt like I had regained her trust.

And then reality hit hard.

Halfway up the hill, it was as if someone flicked a switch. Tan suddenly remembered that she was supposed to be terrified of me and our walks. The PTSD from the rook scarer must have come rushing back in a wave. For no discernible reason, she pivoted on the spot, darted back down the hill, breezed past Layla and me without a second glance, ducked under the gate, and ran straight home.

'TAAAANNN?' called Layla. 'Tan? Please come back!'

'What's going on with her?' I asked. 'It was all going so well.'

'It's classic trauma association,' she said.

Layla is studying psychology at A-Level and likes to analyse our family dynamics and tell us about the psychology behind our various character traits. She's started trying to apply her studies to Tan.

'What does that mean?' I asked.

'It's the conditioning. You're her negative stimulus. She sees you and remembers the loud bangs of the rook scarer. Or you bashing that stupid rock.'

'Alright, you don't need to bring that up again. But she's happy to walk through the field where the rook scarer was. Just not with me.'

'Well, I think Tan has transferred her fear of the rook scarer onto you. It's called 'displacement'.'

'What do I do?'

'You need to do more positive reinforcement.'

'Positive reinforcement? I just took a thorn out of her paw! Surely that should count for something.'

'Yes, but she probably thinks you put it there!'

'That's so stupid.'

'Did you put it there?' she laughed. 'I bet you did.'

Things took an even more confusing turn after that. Tan, who had always been perfectly happy to walk with Layla – including through the field where the rook scarer once stood – suddenly refused to go with her, too. Twice this week, Layla has tried to take her out, and both times Tan wouldn't budge from her kennel.

'What's the psychology behind that then, Layla?' I asked.

Layla seemed temporarily baffled by Tan's recent behaviour.

'Well it's your fault, obviously,' she said.

'How?'

'You've contaminated me by association.'

'What? How?'

'Tan now sees me as the human who lives with you.'

'But you've always lived with me.'

'Yes, but perhaps Tan has only just realised it.'

So now it's not just Tan holding me responsible for her trauma – it's Layla, too.

Far from making progress, it seems we have regressed.

There are other factors at play, though.

Rose, the farm dog who'd occupied the kennel next to Tan's, sadly died last week. She was deaf, mostly blind and of indeterminable age. Four weeks ago, when our friend's dog Rufus came to stay, we had never seen Rose so lively. But she took a sudden turn for the worse last week and the vet was called. Rose passed away before the vet even arrived.

Her death had nothing to do with me.

Rose had been on the farm since Tan arrived as a puppy and has been her constant companion.

Now that Rose is gone, I'm sure Tan feels more vulnerable than ever. We will give her all the time she needs and won't put any pressure on her to join us on walks. She's always welcome on our beach trips – but only if she's comfortable.

Each time I return from our twice-daily walks with Ludo and Milo, I see Tan sitting in her kennel, and it saddens me to think of all the fun she's missing out on. But I have to be patient. There's no rush. I'm confident we'll get back to how things used to be. We'll take it one step at a time, even if that means more false starts than progress.

Make Funny

I'VE ALWAYS ENJOYED INCORPORATING humour into my writing, even when it doesn't belong.

During our school Geography lessons, at the age of 13, I vividly remember our teacher sitting at the front of the class marking the previous week's homework while we worked in silence. It quickly became clear that she was giving each essay no more than a cursory glance. I can't say I blame her – she was overworked, underpaid, and probably bored numb with reading 30 identically dull essays about oxbow lakes and longshore drift. But it made me wonder: why were we spending so long on homework that she didn't even read?

I started slipping random words, phrases, song lyrics and even whole nursery rhymes into my homework, right in the middle of otherwise normal sentences.

It was nerve-wracking watching the teacher mark our homework. What if she suddenly decided to read more closely? Thankfully, she never did. My work would come back with a big tick and a glowing '*Excellent*' or '*Well done*', even though it was littered with these weird additions. It provided great amusement for me and the select few classmates who were in on the secret.

Then there were my two best friends, Mark and Damo (who claims his grandma invented banoffee pie), who were utterly hopeless at French. I wasn't much better, but compared to them, I was practically fluent. Every week, minutes before class, they would beg me to do their homework for them.

I could write whatever I liked, and they would have to hand it in, not having a clue what it said. Sometimes I would be kind and do it properly. Other times, if I was feeling mischievous, I would throw in random phrases like, *'Le dimanche, j'ai mis le feu à la bibliothèque de la ville,'* (*On Sunday, I set fire to the town's library*), or *'Le week-end prochain, je vais danser nue pour quelques centimes sur la place du marché,'* (*Next weekend I am going to be dancing naked for pennies in the market square*). They got some very strange looks from the French teacher.

Later, when I was about 15, a group of us took over the school newspaper. Another tutor group had been writing the monthly publication for a few years, but it was painfully boring, and they sold about 10 copies each month. They were winding it down, so a group of friends and I decided to take it on and give it a revamp.

We got rid of most of the usual columns – the sports match write-ups, the celebrations of pupils' achievements, and the school's new uniform policy. And we replaced it with a completely new format and filled it with things we thought people actually wanted to read. It had an agony aunt column full of made-up problems, articles about the latest music (there was a Blur vs Oasis debate, which is still ongoing 30 years later), and all sorts of other pieces not typical of a school newspaper.

It was an instant hit. We sold out in minutes (probably only about 20 copies, if I'm honest) but had to persuade the lady in charge of reprographics to do some more photocopying.

This was it. We had found our calling.

And then the newspaper got banned.

It was deemed too controversial and too edgy, and the school didn't want to endorse it.

We reached a compromise and toned things down significantly for the second issue, but the magic was gone. We no longer enjoyed writing it, and our readers were equally disappointed by the watered-down version. After that, the paper folded, after just two editions.

Looking back, that school newspaper project was probably my first real experience of writing for an audience. Even though it was short-lived, it gave me a taste of what it's like to have people read and react to your words. I've still got a copy tucked away in the attic somewhere, and one day I'll dig it out for a future post – though I'm sure it'll make for some cringeworthy reading. In hindsight, the teachers were probably right to ban it. I was trying too hard to push boundaries, desperate to be funny, without really knowing how to make it work. I'm still not sure I do.

I no longer try to force humour into my writing. I never think, *'What could I write here to try and make this bit funny?'* or *'How can I squeeze a joke into this section?'*.

If I do, it usually falls flat.

There are times when Rachel reads my draft and leaves notes like *'LOL'* in the margins, even though she was sitting right next to me and definitely didn't. Sometimes she'll mark a section *'MAKE FUNNY'*, which means I should add a joke and inject some humour. It's very rare that I will be able to 'make funny'. Forcing it just doesn't work – it feels contrived. Instead, I take Rachel's note as a polite way of saying, *'This bit is shit.'* So, rather than shoehorn in a joke, I usually rewrite the section or, more often than not, delete it completely.

> tting at
> . It
> n't say I
> ~~ ~~
> were
> read?

Make funny!

Most of the funny bits in my books come from real life – things that happened to me or people I know. I'm just retelling the story. The humour is already there, in the original event. All I'm doing is recounting it.

Of course, I could invent scenarios just to squeeze out a few laughs, but where would it stop? One moment, I'm adding a little drama to spice things up, and the next thing you know, we've got explosions, high-speed car chases, and alien abductions.

Readers are smart though and will sense when something doesn't feel authentic. And once you've lost a reader's trust you are unlikely to gain it back.

Unfortunately for me, some of my real-life stories are so absurd and so ludicrous that people assume I've invented them. Take, for example, these two one-star reviews for *Not Tonight, Josephine* (I should do another post one day sharing my favourite one-star reviews. I've got some absolute gems). Both reviewers thought the idea that Mark and I would have walked 30 miles and bought a car without even switching the engine on was completely ridiculous.

To be fair, it was ridiculous – but it was also true. Still, that level of absurdity was enough for them to lose interest.

★☆☆☆☆ Verified Purchase
A fairy tale
Reviewed in the United Kingdom on 18 December 2016
What a disapontment, I have only read 25% and find it a fairy story, The ridiculous part about buying the car, with his friend offering more money. All ridiculous, however some people did not think so.

★☆☆☆☆
Absurd. Contrived. When they bought the car without ...
Reviewed in the United States on June 25, 2018
Absurd. Contrived. When they bought the car without really seeing it or turning it on I was done. Too ridiculous

I don't necessarily have the best sense of what readers will find funny. There are some parts that make me smile as I write them, but they won't get any reaction whatsoever from Rachel, let alone a '*LOL*' in the margin. Perhaps somebody, somewhere chuckled too, but if not, then at least it amused me.

Very few of my friends subscribe to my weekly Substack newsletter. Even fewer of them actually read my posts. So it was a nice surprise this week when I drove past my friend Rich and he called out to me, 'NOBODY WANTS A COCKCHAFER IN THE BEDROOM,' in reference to last week's story about the Hornet Dilemma. It was reassuring to discover it was not just me laughing at that one.

Then there are other sections where Rachel will write '*LOL*' that I almost got rid of completely because I thought they were rubbish. There's probably a stack of great jokes sitting in my recycle bin that never made it past the first draft.

I do enjoy slipping in a reference to something I've written about earlier. I think it's known as a callback. It's a way of keeping the reader on their toes. They'll only get the joke if they've been paying attention, and it rewards them with that feeling of being in on it. Especially if the callback is to a different book – then only the most loyal readers catch it.

And then I found 50 quid.

Probably the bits that readers find funniest in my books are conversations. I love writing dialogue and find it relatively easy, maybe because it's so natural. You just write down what people have said. You don't have to overthink sentence structure or use fancy words – at least not with the people I know. Real conversations are usually messy, full of interruptions, misunderstandings, and quirks, and that's where the humour lies.

For my first book – *Free Country* – most of the humour comes from my travel companion, Ben. I was fortunate enough to do the trip with one of the funniest people I've ever met. He provided the raw material, and I just retold the story.

Then there's Rachel, who is a regular character in all my other books. She's also one of the funniest people I know, and any email or message I get about how funny she is – or more likely, how much of a saint she is for putting up with me – gets read aloud to her. She'll nod and say, 'Yes, I am very funny, aren't I?' And I just remind her, 'I wrote you!'

My children also provide a lot of the material for my books too. I often just sit back and observe.

I've dug myself in a hole here, haven't I? I've pulled back the curtain and ruined the magic trick. It turns out I'm not funny at all. I'm just surrounded by funny people, stealing their jokes, anecdotes and witty observations, and putting them on the page.

And I'm okay with that. Writing humour doesn't mean you have to be the source of all the jokes. I'm lucky to have such wonderful, funny people in my life, and I'm honoured to be the one who gets to share their humour with you.

WHAT HAPPENS IN POZNAŃ, STAYS IN POZNAŃ...

...AND IN THIS BOOK

It all started with my stag do in 2004. A big group of my friends – some from school, and others from Abington Stanley Football Club – spent three memorable days in Berlin (although a lot of it we can't remember). Over the following years, we went away on each other's stag dos to Barcelona, Ghent, Bochum, and Lisbon.

And then friends stopped getting married.

But we had grown fond of our annual trips away, so continued to go on 'fake stag dos' to various European cities. We visited Bratislava, Ljubljana, Krakow, Madrid, Hamburg plus others.

Our last trip was to Riga, Latvia in 2019, just before the world ground to a halt.

Covid put a stop to our trips in 2020 and 2021, and then life got in the way for the following two years. It felt like our tradition of getaways had reached a natural end.

The Daily Mash – a satirical online news website in the UK – ran an article recently under the headline: ***Existence of entire male friendship group hinges on one vaguely organised bloke.***

This describes our friendship group perfectly.

If it wasn't for Damo (who claims his grandma invented banoffee pie), these trips simply would not happen. Damo has been chief organiser for all of them. All except his own stag do, of course – The Greatest Stag Do That Never Was – that featured in my book *Reconnecting*...

Damo sent out a message at the beginning of this year with a date, a city and a cheap price asking who was keen.

Last weekend, ten of us gathered at London-Luton Airport ready for a weekend in the Polish city of Poznań.

This trip also marked a significant milestone for me. I've been taking a break from alcohol for the last four months, which I wrote about earlier. Back then, I claimed that I hadn't noticed any benefits to giving up alcohol. Had things changed after another two months?

I might write a longer post about this at some point when I have worked out the status of my relationship with alcohol. But, in summary, no, not really. Other than saving a bit of money, I didn't really experience any of the life-changing benefits that non-drinkers rave about.

But I think that my relationship with alcohol has shifted. It doesn't hold the same allure it used to, which must surely be a good thing.

Having said that, I didn't want to be the non-drinker on this trip, so found myself with a pint in hand at the airport at 10.30 am. My first drink in four months.

The beer tasted good, but there wasn't a moment when I thought, 'God, I've missed this.' Especially not during breakfast.

But I had a second one, just to make sure.

We landed in Poznań in the early afternoon and got taxis to our youth hostel, dumped our bags and went off to explore the city. Poznań's Old Town is dominated by the magnificent market square – the Stary Rynek – lined on all four sides by brightly coloured former tenement houses, that are now mostly bars and restaurants.

It felt great to be back with that familiar feeling – same friends, different European city. Some of the group I hadn't seen since 2019, but the beauty of old friends is that we all seamlessly slipped back into taking the piss out of each other like we always used to. While the venue and the language change, the heart of these weekends remains the same. It's not about the destination; it's about reconnecting.

None of our group speaks any Polish. It's a difficult language even to grasp the basics of, but I always try to make an effort in each country we visit, so learned how to say *'good morning'*, *'please'* and *'thank you'*, which is usually just enough to get by.

Every time I ordered beers, food, or had any interaction with someone Polish, I said 'dziękuję' (thank you) pretty much every other word. I got laughed at quite a lot but I think most people seemed to appreciate the effort.

Now that we have all aged and matured (yeah right!) since our last trip, I assumed the drinking would have toned down. I was wrong. We had only been at the first bar five minutes when we bought Damo a 'gift' for organising everything. A cocktail served in a miniature bathtub. That's what friends are for.

As we worked our way from bar to bar around the square, cocktails for the rest of us soon followed, and then a beer taster selection each.

To tide us over until dinner, we ordered ten portions of chips and five baskets of bread at one of the bars. This arrived accompanied with garlic butter, ketchup and mayo, and we assembled our own impromptu chip butties at our outdoor table in the town square.

The waiter was utterly bemused by the sight of ten tourists eating chip sandwiches at his bar. He looked strangely curious, though, and I'm certain he went back to the kitchen and assembled his own. If the chip butty becomes the national dish of Poland, it's all thanks to us.

We then found ourselves in a bar offering 130 different shots for £1.50 each, and, naturally, we sampled more than a few. From then on, we decided everything in Poznań cost £1.50, even when it didn't.

By this point, I was starting to fade. I'd been up since 3:30 am to get to the airport in time, while eight of the other nine lived within an hour of Luton, and therefore managed significantly more sleep – four of them even lazily/wisely stayed at an airport hotel.

The night ended in a kebab shop, but things got a little hazy after that. I do remember saying 'dziękuję' (*thank you*) far too many times.

Earlier that afternoon, when we were still feeling energetic and sprightly, four of us in the group expressed an interest in taking part in Poznań's parkrun on the Saturday morning. Parkrun, for those who don't know, is a series of free, timed 5 km events that take place around the world at 9 am on a Saturday morning. Parkrun began in 2004 in Bushy Park, London (formerly the Bushy Park Time Trial). Twenty years later, there are now over 2,200 organised weekly parkruns around the world in 23 different countries.

Much to my surprise, four of us assembled outside the hostel at 8.30 the following morning, all feeling and looking particularly ropey. Poznań's parkrun takes place in the sprawling Park Cytadela to the north of the city, once the home of a German military fortress – one of the largest in Europe. It was a 20-minute walk to the start and I was slightly concerned I might throw-up or shit myself either before or during the run. The sight of a lone overflowing portable toilet on our way through the park didn't do much to help the situation.

By 8.55 am, about 100 runners and walkers had gathered for the pre-race briefing. One of the organisers noticed us looking a little confused and 'foreign' and kindly gave us a personal briefing in English. I must have said 'dziękuję' to him about 20 times during those five minutes. They could not have been more welcoming and even invited us to join them for breakfast after the event, and gave us a special mention in their pre-race announcement.

The run was a single, winding loop of the park, passing tanks, aeroplanes, and other old war relics. It was my first 5 km event in many years and, being used to longer but MUCH slower runs, I had forgotten how tough it is to run 5 km. Especially with a raging hangover. But the four of us completed it in a respectable time and felt surprisingly better afterwards.

We walked the mile back to our hostel as the rest of our group were all surfacing, and after a quick shower, headed to breakfast in the market square where we unwittingly found ourselves with front-row seats beneath the city's most famous tourist attraction.

Poznań's headbutting goats.

From about 11 am, crowds began to gather next to our table beside the town hall. At noon every day, two mechanical goats emerge from a door at the top of the tower and butt heads.

The tradition began way back in the middle of the 16th century. The town hall had been badly damaged by fire and subsequently rebuilt. During the grand opening, lots of the city's dignitaries were invited for a meal in the square to celebrate the occasion. A young chef named Pietrek was tasked with cooking a venison leg for the guests. He neglected his duties and took a break to go and admire the new building. While he was gone, the venison fell into the fire and was ruined. Pietrek then panicked and ran to a nearby field where locals kept their livestock and stole two goats. He brought them back to the kitchen with the plan to cook them instead. Somehow, Pietrek was even more incompetent than first thought, and the goats escaped. They ran up the stairwell of the town hall's tower and emerged above the turrets and began headbutting each other. The onlookers below found the whole fiasco extremely entertaining.

Pietrek was forgiven for his incompetence as the guests had such a memorable evening, thanks to the goats. And so a craftsman was ordered to create mechanical goats that could replicate this new tradition every day.

The goats were also pardoned, saved from the cooking pot, and returned to the field. It's not known what the guests ate for dinner that night. If only 16th-century Poznań had known about chip butties.

As we sat and ate our breakfast, we could feel the anticipation growing. There were now several hundred people all assembled next to our table, all eyes fixated on the clock tower.

As the first bong of the clock struck midday, there was a loud gasp from the assembled crowd. Many of whom had been waiting for nearly an hour for this spectacle. The wait was finally over.

Right on cue, two mechanical goats emerged from a small door at the top of the clock tower, turned to face each other and then began butting heads.

I wish I could say we were swept away by the drama of it all. But honestly, it was so fucking boring. It was comically dull. But the crowd were loving it. Every single person had their phone pointed towards the goats throughout and were filming the entire 'spectacle', ready to bore others about it later. As I am doing here.

It's a genius marketing ploy, though, and certainly gave a huge tourism boost to the city centre.

After breakfast, which had dragged on into lunch, two of our group went off to watch a division 1 football match between Warta Poznań and Arka Gdynia. They arrived at the stadium just before kick-off to find it was empty. It turns out Warta Poznań's ground didn't meet the league's requirements, so they now play their home games 50 km away. Warta Poznań lost 1-0.

The rest of us wandered around town and found a beach bar in a park. While floods ravaged parts of southern Poland, and the UK was being hit by severe weather, we felt fortunate and privileged to be sitting on deckchairs in the sun.

More bars, cocktails and shots followed, with Polish hot dogs and sauerkraut for lunch, and not-so-Polish burgers for dinner.

At 1 am, five of us found ourselves in a small bar chatting to a bear of a man named Martin. He was about 6ft 5in with the biggest hands I have ever seen.

Poznań's most famous food, before we introduced chip butties to the city, was the St Martin's Croissant – a poppy seed croissant traditionally baked on 11th November (St Martin's Day), although now popular year-round.

'Ah, Martin! Like the croissant?' I said, hoping he would be impressed with my local knowledge.

He glared at me.

'No. Not like the croissant.'

'Oh, ok.'

Brits abroad have a bad reputation. Much of it justified. Martin initially sat looking at us suspiciously across the bar, silently judging us, but eventually pulled his stool over to join us at our table.

As we spent more time asking about his life and showing genuine interest in his stories, Martin began to warm to us. He was a man with his (huge) fingers in many pies: a stuntman, a battle re-enactment enthusiast, a potato farmer, a flower farmer, and the owner of Poznań's potato museum. We talked about potatoes, Poznań's fascinating history, football, the British sitcom *Keeping Up Appearances* (it's how some Polish people learn English, apparently) and the stereotype of Brits abroad. He even taught us a few phrases in Polish, although I mostly stuck to repeating 'dziękuję' every other word.

By the end of the night, Martin seemed surprised to confess that he was wrong, and that some Brits were actually pretty decent people. We parted with big hugs (I was a little worried he was going to crush me), and a promise to come and visit his potato museum next time we are in Poznań.

I ended a very surreal night at 02.34, guessing Wordle in one while sitting on the toilet. I wouldn't have believed (or remembered) it if I hadn't taken a screenshot.

Eager to make the most of our 48 hours in Poznań, the same four who took part in Parkrun, set off for another run at 9 am the following morning – this time around Lake Malta.

Lake Malta is an artificial lake, created by the damming of the Cybina River in 1952, and is now a popular rowing and water-skiing facility. Just not on a Sunday morning. The path around the lake was busy with runners, walkers and cyclists, but there was nobody on the water. The sun was out in full and several times we considered ignoring the many '*no swimming*' signs and jumping in. But after all that effort bolstering Anglo-Polish relations the night before, we didn't want to risk undoing all our good work.

Sunday's run didn't have the same magical healing effects as the previous day and all of us still felt pretty rough afterwards.

Thankfully, we've learned our limits over the years. Back in the day, we'd do three nights, but everyone now agrees that two is plenty. After a coffee, croissant, and some weird bread thing filled with cheese and an unwelcome egg, we headed back to the airport for our return flight.

The pilot had mentioned turbulence, but the flight had been mostly uneventful—until we approached London-Luton. As the plane descended through thick clouds, it began to shake violently, and the runway finally came into view. Just when we were about to touch down, the pilot yanked on the joystick and hit the thrusters and turbo boosters (that's the official aviation lingo, right?), sending us climbing steeply back into the sky. There were gasps and shrieks throughout the cabin – though, to be fair, not quite as many as we heard for the goats. The pilot then calmly explained over the PA that the conditions were too dangerous for landing and that we'd be doing a 'go-around.'

He then added one of the scariest sentences I've ever heard in my life:

'So, we will fly around for a bit and then I'll have another crack at it.'

This is not what you want to hear from the only person capable of getting you all to the ground alive. I don't fly very often (three flights in the last five years) and I've become a more anxious passenger as I've got older. But a weirdly calm acceptance washed over me. It was a situation completely out of my control and all I could do was hope for the best. And I was reassured that the pilot was at least going to have another crack at it.

After circling through the clouds for another 15 minutes, we descended again and this time touched down on the runway, albeit with heavy contact, skidded a little and then the plane eventually came to a stop.

But the journey wasn't over.

I still had a five-hour drive back to Devon. And to complicate things further, all access to the airport was blocked by a flooded tunnel, leaving us stranded. No cars or buses could get in or out. So we ended up walking nearly a mile to intercept a rogue shuttle bus and somehow convinced the driver to turn back and take us to the car park. When we finally reached the car park, it was underwater. We waded to our cars and said our goodbyes, over 2.5 hours later than planned.

I made it home just before midnight, after three days and two nights of far too little sleep, far too much to drink, and experiencing the kind of overall fatigue that seriously makes you question your life choices.

These weekends are more than just an excuse to drink or explore a new city. They're about keeping valuable friendships alive that might otherwise fade under the pressure of distance, time, and the chaos of life. It's in the shared laughter, relentless piss-taking, inside jokes, and half-remembered adventures that you realise why these people are so important, even after all these years.

Which is why, despite the hangovers and the long journey home, I'm already looking forward to next year's trip.

Lessons Learned from Ten Years as a Full-Time Author

And One Year on Substack

This month marks a couple of big milestones for me.

Firstly, it's my TENTH anniversary as a full-time author (*woo-hoo!*). I published my first book in May 2012, and by October 2014, I had officially ended my career as a photographer.

Secondly, it's been a year since I started my weekly posts on Substack (another *woo-hoo!*). So, what better time to reflect on what I've learned along the way?

Writing is hard – and I'm one of the lucky ones

Very few people write a book and manage to make a career out of it. I get that, and I (try to) remind myself daily what a fortunate position I am in. But 'lucky' doesn't mean it's been easy – far from it.

You would think that after 17 books, I would have this shit figured out. But each one is just as difficult as the last. What I have learned, though, is that knowing it's going to be hard makes the process slightly less daunting. But only very slightly. I still feel a sense of dread and self-doubt each time I stare at a blank page as I begin a new book or Substack post.

The productivity myth

I am incredibly lazy. I have published 17 books in 12 years. To many people – people with proper jobs – that sounds prolific. *How do you write so much? Where do you find the time?* If you break it down, though, it works out as about 150 words a day. I'm not exactly a writing machine. I waste a lot of time, and procrastination is my constant companion. I like to think it's part of the creative process. It's really not, but I'll keep pretending it is.

Writing is the easy part

If you've ever written a book – or even tried – you'll know it's bloody difficult. But compared to trying to sell your book, writing is genuinely the easy part. The market is more saturated than ever, algorithms are becoming more complex, marketing opportunities are shrinking while getting more expensive, and readers' attentions are being pulled in a thousand different directions. With so many distractions, getting your book noticed often feels like an impossible challenge.

I still don't call myself a writer

I am still intimidated by the word 'writer' and never refer to myself as one. I rarely call myself an author either. Being a writer implies I know what I'm doing (I don't), and being an author implies someone else trusts that I know what I'm doing (they don't). When people ask what I do, I tell them, 'I write books.' Because no matter how bad my writing, or how few people read my words, I *do* write books, so that's what I stick with.

I'd rather people not know

If I had my way, nobody I know would read anything I've written. Friends, family, neighbours – I'd prefer they stay blissfully unaware of my work.

Thankfully, most of them are.

My books aren't available at my local bookshop, and that's the way I like it. Nothing against local bookshops – I *love* local bookshops and would like nothing more than for my books to be available on their shelves. Just not the shelves of MY local bookshop. I much prefer selling to readers I've never met – there's less awkwardness that way.

I'm bad at predicting what will sell

I am really bad at predicting which books and which posts will do well, and which won't.

I reluctantly published *Not Tonight, Josephine* thinking very few people would read it. It has become my best-selling book in its time. Conversely, I was convinced *The Self-Help Bible* would be my most commercially successfully. Hardly anyone has read it.

It's the same with Substack, I almost didn't publish the post about *The Cat Next Door*, because, well, it's basically just a load of photos of a cat, but readers seemed to love it (I should have known. Cute cat pics! Duh!). Other posts that I thought would really resonate seemed to fall flat.

I've got high hopes for this one ...which is probably a bad sign.

But I've learned to see failure as part of the process. You have to take risks to grow, and sometimes that means failing.

Writing is a lonely pursuit

As a photographer, I spent a lot of time with people – even if I wasn't building lifelong bonds, there was at least interaction. As a writer of books, there's almost nothing. I have become more introverted and more socially awkward and have to force myself to actively seek out human interaction to keep me sane.

It's not all doom and gloom. I've made some incredible friends and connections over the years through writing. It's a really supportive community (especially on Substack) where people truly understand the ups and downs of this strange way of life. I've learned so much from those who generously share their insights and experience, and I try to do the same whenever I can.

Learn from others – without envy

It's easy to compare myself to more successful authors and feel deflated. But I've learned to let those doing better than me inspire me, rather than demoralise me. Sometimes I forget that to many, I'm one of the successful ones. It's funny how perspective works.

Don't expect financial stability

If you're after financial security or a steady paycheque, don't become an author. This career is a financial rollercoaster. To illustrate this rollercoaster, I thought I would share my royalty graph for the last 12 years.

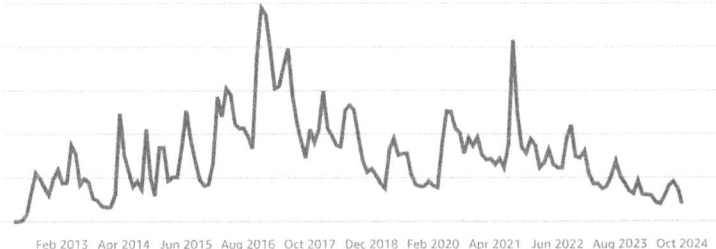

[Graph showing fluctuating line from Feb 2013 to Oct 2024]

Feb 2013　Apr 2014　Jun 2015　Aug 2016　Oct 2017　Dec 2018　Feb 2020　Apr 2021　Jun 2022　Aug 2023　Oct 2024

As the graph above illustrates, success in this field comes in waves. You have to ride them without getting too cocky on the peaks or too disheartened by the troughs. The trick is to stay afloat, keep paddling, and hope the next big one rolls in soon. And when it does, you'd better be ready to catch it.

I'm ready! Any day now, surely?

Regrets?

I have no regrets about taking the leap from my previous career to write full-time. It's extremely tough, lonely, and financially unrewarding, but I wouldn't want it any other way.

Well, apart from all of those ways.

Readers are everything

If it weren't for readers – whether you've picked up one of my books or discovered my writing online – I wouldn't be here. Your role is crucial. Whether it's reviews, ratings, recommendations to friends and family, or simply engaging with what I write, it all makes a massive difference. Not just for my ego (well, a little bit for my ego), but mostly because it helps my work reach more people.

Substack has been a whole new learning curve

Speaking of engaging with readers, my experience writing on Substack has been an entirely new challenge. The process is different from working on a book – even though much of what I write there often finds its way into one. There's more immediacy, and the feedback loop is tighter. I get to see, almost in real-time, what resonates with people and what falls flat.

And it's been refreshing. As I said above, writing is inherently antisocial, but Substack has been a bridge between this solitary work and real-time connection with readers. It has helped me feel less isolated in this unpredictable and often lonely career.

The future? Uncertain, but I'm not done yet

Will I still be writing books in another ten years? It's hard to say. I hope so. But the publishing landscape has changed dramatically in recent years and will continue to shift faster than ever. The future of books is very uncertain. AI is here to stay, and it won't be long before robot-written books become common and widely accepted. Writing non-fiction might give me an edge for a while longer, but I know I won't be able to compete with the machines forever.

But for now, I'll keep writing as long as I have something to say – and as long as you're here to read it.

To those of you who've been reading my books for years, thank you for sticking with me. And to those just discovering me, welcome – I hope this is the start of a long journey together. Your support, whether recent or long-standing, means the world.

All of the stories in this book were first published as part of my Substack newsletter, *Reconnecting...* between April and October 2024.

Stay Connected with Reconnecting...

THANK YOU FOR CHOOSING to read my book. If you enjoyed it, I would be extremely grateful if you would consider posting a short review wherever you bought your copy and help spread the word about my books in any way you can.

By joining my Substack newsletter, *Reconnecting...*, you can stay up-to-date with all my latest posts and receive news about upcoming books and projects. There are two ways to subscribe:

- **Free Subscription**: As a free subscriber, you'll receive occasional public posts and stay informed about any big news and new book releases.

- **Paid Subscription**: By becoming a paid subscriber, you'll receive regular brand new stories from me, plus access to the full archive (including my audio narration). You will also receive exclusive bonus content, plus a free ebook copy of each new anthology volume as its released.

Whether you choose to sign up as a *free* or *paid* subscriber, I truly appreciate you being there.

To subscribe, simply visit:
georgemahood.substack.com

You can also keep in touch via social media:
Facebook: @georgemahood
Instagram: @georgemahood
TikTok: @georgemahood
Twitter/X: @georgemahood

I have published many other books. Please read on...

Reconnecting...
Tales of adventure, travel and life

GEORGE MAHOOD

Also by George Mahood

- Free Country: A Penniless Adventure the Length of Britain

- Every Day Is a Holiday

- Life's a Beach

- Operation Ironman: One Man's Four Month Journey from Hospital Bed to Ironman Triathlon

- Not Tonight, Josephine: A Road Trip Through Small-Town America

- Travels with Rachel: In Search of South America

- How Not to Get Married: A no-nonsense guide to weddings... from a photographer who has seen it ALL

- Did Not Finish: Misadventures in Running, Cycling and Swimming

- The Self-Help Bible: All the Answers for a Happier, Healthier Life

- Things I'd Tell My Teenage Self: A Toolkit for Life

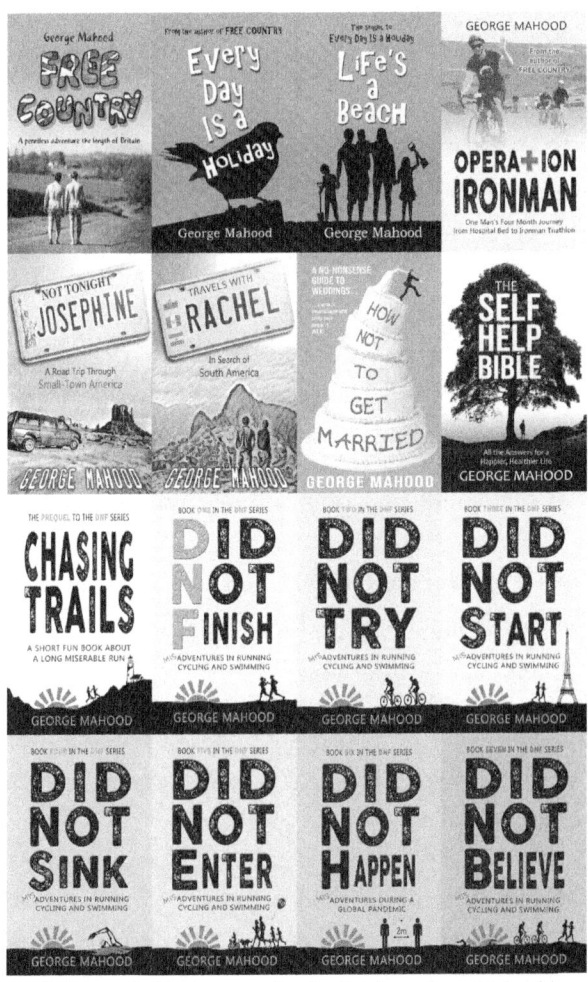

(all available in paperback, ebook and audiobook)

Acknowledgements

A BIG THANK YOU to Sue and Becky, my two amazing proofreaders. If there are any errors left, they're entirely my fault – most likely added after you finished. Please check out Becky's fab book blog, Bookaholic Bex.

To my wife, Rachel, thanks for all your *'lol'* and *'make funny'* feedback. To my children, Layla, Leo, and Kitty: thank you for letting me borrow bits of our lives and share them with the world (not that you're ever likely to read this).

To my Substack subscribers, you have been an unexpected but incredible addition to my writing journey. When I started posting there in October 2023, I wasn't sure what to expect. Your encouragement and support mean more than I can express. The idea that so many of you believe in my work as a worthy investment continues to blow me away.

A special shout-out to all my paid subscribers – it's your support that has made this book possible. As a token of my appreciation, I have listed your names here. If I've missed anyone, please let me know – thank you!

Ali Lawrence, Amy Brown, Andrea Beauchamp, Ania, Ann Fernan, Ann Perno, AnnMarie, Anu Itty, Barbara Berney, Barbara Hibberd, Becky Muth, Bert, Bill, Brad Ryder, Bridget jones, C A, Carol A Murray, Caroline, Caryn Rybczynski, Catherine Pearce, Chasw, Cheri, Cheryl F, Chris D, Christine Barbour, Colleen, Connie Miranda, Courtney, Dave Catling, Dave Hunt, David Rice, Debs Mutton, Deby, Dee, Demelza Booth, Denise Rogers, Dennis Ward, Diane Clapes, Diane Hart, Don Guyton, Elaine Clohessy, Elayne, Eline Armstrong, Elizabeth Rodd, Eric Grant, Fiona Davis, Fiona Dennis, Fiona Parker, Florence Bradbury, Fran, Francis Frazzledate, Gayle Tenbrink, Gill Williams, Graeme Scoot, Greg

Grenier, Gwen Desselle, Hayley Marsh, Heather, Heather Fairbank, Helen Jackson, Helen Stenlake, Helena Azzam, Henri ter Steeg, Ian Morris, Izaak Rohman, Jackie Bourne, James B Maas, James Pike, Jamie Craig, Jan Grant Schein, Jane Berrisford, Jane Mahood, Jane Holmes, Janet Nardoni, Jaton West, Jeanne B, Jeanne Barnhill, Jennifer Brodzik, Jenny Hallett, JM Schweikert, Jo Linney, Jodi, Joe Geoghegan, John Lapthorn, John Mahood, John Nelson, Joyce Banker, Judy Fialko, Judy Snow, Julian Sansum, Karen Koch, Kate Allison, Kate Blinick, Kathi Johnson, Keith Davis, Kim, Kirby Snowden, Kirsten Alexander, Kristin Timm, Kristin, Laraine Turk, Laura, Linda Greenlese Mekeel, Linda Purviance, Lisa Correll, Liz Kataras, Liz Salmon, Lizzie, Lori Robson, Loriann, Lorraine Bennett, Lucille Bell, Lucy Hall, Lyn Alban, Lynn Everson, Mara Ostler, Margaret Henderson, Margaret McKee Cooper, Margaret R Lessor, Margaret Thompson, Marianne Phillips, Mark Bradbury, Mary Ritchie, Matthew Ramsey, Michael C. Huntley, Michael, Mike Bruce, Miranda Hall, Morag, Nathalie Boisvert, Nathaniel, Olga Danes-Volkov, Otto A Rosenzweig, Peggy Jacobs, Perla Lovejoy, Petal, Philip Oakley, Rachel Travis, Randall Chancellor, Rashas Weber, Rich, Rich Morrell, Richard Harrison, Rob Metcalf, Robert Bailey, Roberta Villalobos, Robin Fox, Robin Higgins, Rosalynn Bartlett, Ruth Mason, Sally Parker-Yap, Sandy Mata, Sarah F, Shairon, Sharon, Sharon Ayris, Sharon, Sian Griffiths, Sonia, Steph Kelly, Steve Snow, Steven Munsalino, Sue Hewitson, Sue Engel, Susan Dempsey, Susie Folkerts, Suzanne Cochrane, Tim Lawrence, Tracy Bailey, Vanessa, Victoria Livingston

Printed in Great Britain
by Amazon